THE
SURVIVOR

Peter Tadman

GORMAN & GORMAN LTD.

Publishers of Fine Canadian Books
Box 460, Hanna, Alberta T0J 1P0
Telephone (403) 854-3366 — (403) 627-3252

Typesetting and book design by
The Hanna Herald.
Printed and Bound in Canada.

Peter Tadman,
"THE SURVIVOR"
Includes Index —
ISBN: 0-921835-16-7

DEDICATION

To everyone who is a part of this true story.

To those who believed in the importance of an historical documentation of a tragedy that captured global attention.

To Davidie (David) Kootook who was an inspiration in that he wanted his friends to know what had happened. The airplane fell. He ran out of writing paper. Then — he ran out of time. Throughout it all, he was a hero.

To those with the courage of their convictions who do what they think is honestly right.

ACKNOWLEDGEMENTS

Recognition must go to former Toronto Sun reporter Rhona Kane. Wherever you are, Rhona, your contribution to this non-fiction work is not forgotten.

Thank you Dave Reidie, Steve Makris and the Edmonton Journal for allowing use of the best and most complete photographic record available. The picture of nurse Judy Hill was provided through the courtesy of Judge Philip Ketchum and is greatly appreciated.

To all of you who saw the merit of a journalistic record and who were willing to share information in the interests of accuracy, thank you.

Finally, a special thank you to Marten Hartwell for your graciousness towards me during our unexpected, pleasant meeting in the North. Realizing that you sold your story to the Observer and that you and Susan Haley contemplated pursuing a book, I truly felt that you deserved an opportunity to take a direct part in this writing. Your desire not to become involved to that degree is understood and respected. Speaking of respect, David Kootook — as you are fully cognizant — is unable to express his feelings on the subject. I might add though, that you along with the readers of this chronicle should understand that you have gained a great deal of it from those who have come to know you since those frightening, regrettable days.

INTRODUCTION

Reporter Peter Tadman had just returned to Canada via the United States after tracking an accused murderer to Curitiba, Brazil. He reached the suspect before investigators from Interpol, the international police agency, who were also searching for the alleged killer. As a result of his interview, the Attorney General's Department did not pursue Luiz Elizaldo Gonzalves.

Upon arrival, the newsman learned through bold headlines and an accompanying story, of an injured pilot who — incredibly — had survived for 32 days in the freezing Arctic wilderness. Reportedly, the man had lived solely by eating rations and food off the land.

After leaving the airport, Tadman stopped at a nearby shopping centre. By chance, he passed an acquaintance who was a police officer on patrol.

On that cold, snowy night, with car windows rolled down in the middle of the deserted parking lot, the conversation went like this:

Tadman — "I can't believe that with all of those injuries he was able to survive by normal means, there has to be more to it."

Policeman — "Peter, check it out ... it isn't right."

What follows is the true story of Marten Hartwell — THE SURVIVOR.

Part One

THE AIRPLANE FELL

THE SURVIVOR

1

The silver aircraft appeared just before nightfall, the sound of its engines drumming out across the snowbound, desolate wastes.

On the face of it, it was a commonplace sight. In winter, the Canadian Northwest Territories is a bleak, formidable land. Sparsely populated with a mere 53,000 inhabitants — the majority of whom are natives and use their aboriginal tongue as their first language — its vastness stretches for more than 1,300,000 miles across the top of the continent. It is a lonely place, covered for much of the year by snow. No comforting rail line spirals across the great white spaces. There is no ribbon of roads.

In such a land, flying is the lifeline. Bush planes such as this one shuttle across it daily, winging between isolated camps and settlements to ferry in equipment, people and supplies.

This particular craft was a Beech 18, a small, sturdy plane owned by Gateway Aviation.

It had left Yellowknife, the Territorial capital, that morning under routine charter to a mining engineer. Now, due to coincidence and an unforeseen emergency, along with admitted reluctance on the part of the pilot, it would soon attempt a return flight.

The mining engineer, David Thomas of Calgary, along with a member of an oil service drilling crew, had been bound for Swan Lake, a remote camp not far from Perry River on the Arctic coast. The Beechcraft had been chartered to take the men there on the previous day but owing to bad weather they had been forced to return to Yellowknife.

On that morning, they had decided to make a second try. At first, all seemed to go well. But then, they again encountered bad weather, this time in the form of icing conditions and a low cloud ceiling. On the journey out, pilot Marten Hartwell managed to circumvent this by taking the plane through the clouds and riding atop them. By the time they reached Perry River, however, the icing was getting worse and the weather had once again closed in. Visibility was so poor that even though they circled for half-an-hour they were unable to see the outpost where the plane was scheduled to touch down.

By this time, fuel was getting low. Rather than continue indefinitely in this waiting pattern, the pilot decided to continue on across Queen Maud Gulf to Cambridge Bay, on Victoria Island. In addition to refuelling facilities, the settlement had an air weather station where the Perry River forecast could be checked in advance. If the weather remained bad they could stay overnight on the island and complete the trip the following day, this time with full fuel tanks.

Hartwell brought the small plane down without difficulty on the narrow landing strip at Cambridge Bay. As he taxied to a halt outside the refuelling hut, he saw a slight, parka-clad figure scurrying across the windswept tarmac towards him. Cutting the motor, he climbed out. Behind him, he heard groans of relief as David Thomas and his companion gingerly unfolded aching limbs after five cramped hours in the air.

As the individual in the parka drew closer, Hartwell saw that it was a nurse assigned to the Northern Regions medical outpost at the settlement.

There are many nursing stations scattered throughout the Arctic, some of them no bigger than a one-room infirmary. Cambridge Bay, with 10 beds for in-patients, plus a small outpatient clinic, was one of the larger ones. There were three resident nurses, plus a doctor, all posted here by the Canadian Department of National Health & Welfare. In addition to Cambridge Bay, the physician was responsible for six other medical venues and he rotated his duties among them. On this particular day he was attending to patients in Gjoa Haven, on King William Island, miles away.

In the doctor's absence, Ann Budd, a State Registered Nurse from England, was in charge of the nursing station. It was common knowledge in the North that although well-equipped with drugs and nursing aids, the far-flung medical premises did not include surgery facilities. In the event of an emergency, or when an operation was warranted, the patient was simply placed on a plane and ferried to Yellowknife, 535 miles away.

According to the long-legged, businesslike young nurse who had come striding across the tarmac to confront the pilot, such an emergency was now at hand.

Earlier that afternoon, Ann Budd had received a radio alert from Judy Hill, a nurse stationed in the tiny, 350-member community of Spence Bay, on the Boothia Peninsula. Two patients were critically ill and required urgent hospitalization. One was an Inuit woman, Mrs. Neemee Nulliayok, 25, who was eight months pregnant and suffering from premature labor complications. It was her fourth pregnancy and two of them had been failures. The other, her 14-year-old nephew, Davidie (David) Pessurajak Kootook, was vomiting and suffering from severe abdominal pains — in other words, all the symptoms of acute appendicitis. His identification number, given to the Inuit by the authorities, was E4-828. He had never been away from home before.

The pilot of a Twin Otter, another Gateway plane which had been under charter to a water survey crew in the region, was transporting the nurse and patients as far as Cambridge Bay. They would be arriving at any moment. The problem now, Ann Budd explained to Hartwell, was to arrange an airlift as far as Yellowknife.

It was a difficult situation. Hartwell did not want to return to Yellowknife immediately. Yet in the North, there is a strong 'friends and neighbors' policy. People depend upon each other and in an emergency, few will fail to respond. Bush pilots, in particular, will help if at all possible, even flying hundreds of miles out of their way if the situation demands. It is a tradition in this part of the world, and a logical one. For they in turn never know when they will need shelter or food or help.

Hartwell explained to Nurse Budd that he was still under charter. He had put in at Cambridge Bay simply to refuel and he was waiting for the weather to clear so that he could take his passengers back to Perry River. Rather than decide on the spot, Hartwell had agreed to wait until the other plane came in. Afterall, as the nurse pointed out, it was a matter of life and death.

The Twin Otter DHC6, piloted by Ed Logozar, touched down 10 minutes later. While Nurse Hill and an accompanying pediatrician, Dr. Ernest McCoy, transferred the patients to a waiting station wagon and from there to the warmth of the nursing station, the two pilots discussed who would make the trip. Once she was sure they understood the urgency of the situation, Ann Budd left them to it. Returning to the station, she went to the kitchen to pack up a lunch for Judy Hill. As far as she was concerned, it did not matter which pilot took over the medical evacuation. The important thing was to get the passengers out.

Out on the landing strip, Hartwell and Logozar compared charters. The Twin Otter, which had heavy hydrographic equipment aboard, was scheduled to go on to Coppermine. As the weather in Perry River was still bad, and Hartwell stranded in Cambridge Bay for the night anyway, the Beechcraft seemed the logical choice for the mercy flight. The German-born pilot was still hesitant. He had not been pleased about the icing conditions on the morning run. However, it was true that the Beechcraft was a bit faster than the Twin Otter and since it carried an hour's extra fuel, it did have a lot more range. Beyond that, as Logozar stressed, it would even be possible to go to Yellowknife and be back in Cambridge Bay that same night. It was an approximate three and one-half-hour flight.

Far from being overjoyed at the prospect, but seeing no viable alternative, Hartwell agreed. The mining engineer consented to releasing the charter and the pilot would take the patients to Yellowknife. Once there, however, he would want to have a good night's rest and only return to Cambridge Bay the following morning.

The matter settled, Logozar helped unload a barrel type container and an oil pump from the Beechcraft, then left to complete preparations for the next leg of his own journey.

Hartwell refuelled his plane himself, adding 172 gallons to the 30 gallons still remaining in the tanks. While waiting for the nurse and the two patients to arrive, he went into the air weather station to check the forecast and file his flight plan.

2

In the late afternoon of November 8, 1972, the twin engined Beechcraft 18 took off from the secluded settlement of Cambridge Bay.

Aboard were the two seriously ill patients and their nurse, Judith Ann Hill, 27. Nurse Hill had come to Canada from the small South Devon town of Kingsbridge after training in England. The dedicated, determined young woman chose to be posted to the Arctic after initially practicing her profession in the Atlantic and Prairie regions of her new found country. Judy Hill was highly regarded. She was outgoing, full of life and extremely strong-willed.

The pilot was Marten Hartwell, 47. He was a former glider pilot for the Hitler Youth. He was also a former member of the German Luftwaffe who had resumed his flying career when he emigrated to Canada alone in 1967. Hartwell had been on the Gateway payroll for the past six months. Previously he had flown in northern Manitoba where he had experienced a minor crash.

Under normal circumstances, he enjoyed the job. It was a free life and an adventurous one. Admittedly, the hours were long and flying conditions were far from perfect. In fact, once in the air, it was a constant battle against ice and snow or the gale-force winds that came howling down from the nearby North Pole. But at least he was in the pilot's seat. Hartwell had spent 20 years trying to get work in the aviation wasteland that was post-war Germany. In the end, he had left for Canada. But the frustrating taste of that time was still too close to forget.

At the moment, however, he was not feeling particularly cheerful.

Keeping one ear tuned to the crackling radio transmitter of CF-RLD, he peered out with distrust at the gathering dusk. Before him lay the Barren Lands, an immense white desert of Arctic tundra stretching out to the distance in endless, foreboding miles. It was not a reassuring sight. Crossing this region could be hazardous even at the best of times. The people of the North had a name for it. They called it the Land of Lost Planes.

On this trip, the first flicker of alarm had come at 3:34 p.m., barely a minute after he had lifted off. Brian McBurney, the Ministry of Transport (MOT) radio operator at Cambridge Bay, had called to query the fact that there had been no mention of an ambulance on the flight plan. Did he want one to be waiting for the patients when they arrived in Yellowknife? Hartwell had promptly signalled back yes, but he had to repeat himself, again and again. McBurney had difficulty reading his reply.

Now that he had passed Bathurst Inlet, however, the pilot felt more reassured.

He looked over his shoulder. The patients were tranquil. Wrapped in sleeping bags, they were laying on two stretchers that had been placed in the back of the plane. The pregnant woman was on the left of the craft with the boy beside her. From time to time, the nurse would go back to check on them. He glanced over to the co-pilot's seat, where the tall, blonde girl in the hooded blue parka sat staring out at the edge of night. Apart from the routine exchange of courtesies at Cambridge Bay, while the patients were being placed on board, they had not spoken. The constant drone of the engine filled the tiny cockpit, making conversation difficult. Besides, it was no time to be sociable. The young nurse was obviously pre-occupied with her sick charges and if they were to make good time to Yellowknife, he had enough work on his hands.

By 5:10 p.m., they had been airborne for one hour and 37 minutes. They were crossing Contwoyto Lake and once more, the pilot's attention was riveted to the radio.

Situated on an island in the lake, the Contwoyto beacon was used regularly by northern pilots as a means of determining their course and position during flights between Cambridge Bay and the Territorial capital. Hartwell had been trying to do this, in turn. But in spite of several attempts, he had been unable to get a clear signal. It was puzzling, since he believed the Beechcraft could not have been passing more than 15 to 20 miles from the island beacon. But in this case, he was not overly concerned. The beacon was a low-powered one and he had concluded on previous trips that he could not always rely on it.

It was getting darker now and the small aircraft was hurtling into a twilight world. On his right, Judy Hill seemed to have fallen asleep. The patients too, for there was no sound nor movement from the rear.

As the Beechcraft was heading southwest, it was catching up with the sunset. There was still light and clearer skies about 45 degrees to the right, and pieces of open sky were visible through the clouds. To the east, however, the inhospitable Barren Lands lay shrouded in shadow.

Hartwell was reaching again towards the radio when a flicker of movement on the instrument panel caught his eye. It was the compass, the needle swirling like a dervish behind the glassed-in-dial. He had been expecting it. Nevertheless, it was an unsettling sight.

A 17 mile per hour tail wind had begun to blow from the east and once again, he regretted the trouble with the gyro. He continued to persevere with the radio, trying to get direction indications from beacons further ahead on his flight path. The reception, however, was not good. All he was picking up were signals from Fort Reliance, way over to the west, and from Fort

Franklin.

If Hartwell was now beginning to feel anxious, it was not through any fears of getting lost. He knew that there was at least six hour's worth of fuel aboard the Beechcraft and he was confident that sooner or later he would manage to zero-in on Yellowknife. With the two sick passengers on board, his main concern was to not lose time. As the nurse had underscored, the clock was already working against these patients. At this point, extra minutes ticking away could well mean the difference between life and death.

Perhaps if he lost altitude, he would have better luck. Otherwise, without a signal, he would wind-up twisting in circles for half-an-hour or more.

With eyes straining to see into the gloom, he realized that he did not have many options left. Darkness was closing in with a vengeance now and the cramped interior of the Beechcraft was lost in shadow. One thing was certain. He would have to act soon. He could not go on like this forever, for now he was flying blind.

In the small, cramped waiting room at the Yellowknife airport, the ambulance driver again picked-up his tattered copy of the News of the North. He was beginning to know it by heart. He had been waiting for more than an hour and there was nothing else to fill the time.

Every so often, more as an excuse to stretch his legs than anything else, he wandered over to the information counter. But there was nothing new to be learned on the mercy plane's arrival. The tower was still awaiting radio communication from the pilot.

Shortly after 8 p.m., there was a sudden flurry of activity between the information desk and the airport manager's office. It was another 10 to 15 minutes before the official statement was given out.

No word had been received from the Gateway Beechcraft 18 since it had passed Bathurst Inlet, almost four hours before. Since it was now seriously overdue at Yellowknife, and there was still no sign of it, the aircraft had been officially reported as missing. All private and commercial planes in the vicinity were being alerted and the automatic search procedures for lost aircraft would now go into effect.

The ambulance attendant returned to his newspaper. If the plane had just gone off course, or been having radio trouble, there was still a possibility that it could come limping in. He decided to wait for a while. You never can tell in the North but it seemed abundantly clear that the plane with its cargo of sick passengers had simply disappeared.

THE NURSE — Judy Hill. The press called her, "Angel of the Snow."

3

When the emergency flight failed to appear in Yellowknife, an alarm went out to the Edmonton headquarters of the Canadian Armed Forces Search and Rescue Squadron.

Captain Fred Siminoski, with the Rescue Co-ordination Centre at the Namao base in Alberta, took the call at 8:35 p.m. He was told of those aboard and that the pilot, "faded from Cambridge, on course, 71 miles out." Siminoski then called Northern Region headquarters in Yellowknife to discover that the two Twin Otter aircraft were already out. The Royal Canadian Mounted Police (RCMP) were then asked to do a track crawl. It was a few hours later that the Hercules aircraft moved in.

By daylight of the following day, the search for the missing plane was already well underway. Military Hercules and Twin Otters scoured the route that the mercy flight was supposed to have taken, eventually expanding to cover a 100-mile radius on either side. It was known as, "the envelope of probability." All planes were tuned into the North emergency radio frequency in an attempt to pick up signals from the transmitter device known to be aboard the aircraft that had now become invisible.

This was the land of no return. Many aircraft go down in the

Arctic each year. This case, however, was different. The fact that the aircraft had been on an emergency mission, with seriously ill patients on board, captured public concern. Residents of Yellowknife turned out by the score to offer their services as spotters. By the end, 300 of them had contributed their time and their knowledge of the region to look for the silver Beech 18. It was long, frigid work. People were strapped onto the floor of the massive Hercules planes so that they could observe through the opened back door of the craft.

Twenty clairvoyants from across the country offered their services and one seer telephoned Ottawa from the United Kingdom to contribute advice.

Costing in excess of one million dollars, it was the most expensive search in Canadian Aviation history.

After three weeks, convinced that they had covered all possibilities, the Armed Forces called off its mission.

At this time, few people outside the North were aware of the search. Judy Hill's family in England had been contacted by the Northern Region Medical Services and was waiting patiently for news. The Inuit families had also been told. In Yellowknife, Hartwell's girlfriend, 23-year-old Susan Haley, had served as one of the volunteer spotters aboard the military planes. A graduate student at the University of Alberta in Edmonton, she had flown to the small northern capital as soon as the plane was reported missing. She was accompanied by her mother, Mrs. Charlotte Haley of Wolfville, Nova Scotia.

There were some northerners who wanted the search resumed. Little, however, had appeared in the press. This negligence was soon to be corrected in the person of Professor David Haley, Susan's father and the Head of the Mathematics Department, at Acadia University in Nova Scotia.

In a long, detailed letter sent to newspapers across Canada, Professor Haley condemned the cancellation of the search and launched a scathing attack on inefficient, out-of-date equipment and procedures used by the official Armed Forces Rescue Squadron. He was convinced that some of the Beechcraft passengers might still be alive and he quoted his own mathematical calculations to prove it. In all, he spent about $2,000 of his own money in his single-handed attempt to get the search resumed. He also cabled and wrote to Members of Parliament, the Minister of Defence, and even the Prime Minister, Pierre Elliot Trudeau.

He appeared on television and was interviewed by the press and radio reporters across the country. Before long, controversy was bubbling. Were search-and-rescue methods useless? Had the passengers on board the missing Beechcraft been abandoned to certain death?

Whether because of his efforts or not, the tracking was officially restarted three days later on the order of new Minister of Defence, James Richardson.

The Armed Forces had staunchly defended its efforts. As for Haley, he was now a public figure. Some wondered about the underlying reason for his extreme energy in waging his campaign for resumption of the search. Granted, he had met Hartwell and thought he was a fine man. Granted too, his daughter Susan was distraught. But to go to such lengths? One thing was obvious, apart from the human interest involved, many people were now extremely anxious for the plane to be found.

So the search was on again. Once more the planes of the Armed Forces Search and Rescue team took to the air, once again crossing and recrossing the unfriendly territory in hope of a signal or a sign. They also tried new things, such as following the Arctic coastline in case Hartwell had tried to use it as a landmark to find his bearings. They even followed river banks way off his flight course just to be sure.

On December 7th, a military transport on a regular flight from Inuvik, on the Mackenzie River Delta, to Yellowknife, picked up a faint signal from a crash radio beacon. It was one day short of a month from the time that the drama began.

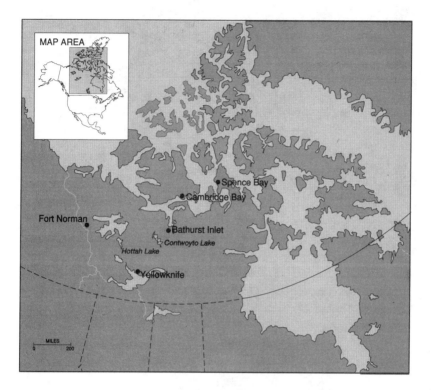

THE TERRITORY — The crash location, near Hottah Lake, was 180 miles off course.

UNREACHABLE LAKE — It could be seen from the air by rescuers and from the land by those occupants of the plane who initially survived. It was 12 miles from the crash site and its fish offered a source of food. It might as well have been 1,000 miles away. They could not reach it.

4

On December 9th, two Hercules, an Argus and a Twin Otter again took to the air. Hercules 326 located a Beaver aircraft which was still on an unexpired flight plan. Determining there were no problems with the Beaver, the Herc crew was then instructed to join the other search units. It was almost at this exact moment that the breakthrough came. Hercules 325, piloted by Captain Ken Moody, had spotted something. It was 48 hours after the distant signal had been heard. Its radio crackled to life.

The survivor at first did not believe his lonely vigil was nearing an end. As he huddled in the makeshift tent for protection he heard what sounded like the howl of a wild beast. The growls became louder and it sounded like more than one animal. Perhaps even a pack. Painfully, he crawled out into the land that had become his prison.

The grumbling had come from above and now down below someone was waving a flare. There was at least one survivor. It seemed incredible! A miracle! The Herc crew, now hovering directly over the crash site, could not positively identify the wreckage. There was uncertainty, but it did appear that the debris was the remains of the Beech 18. It was 10:40 a.m.

There was an immediate flurry of activity in the search and

rescue headquarters as Captain Keith Gathercole began redirecting the remaining search units. Captain Ken Moody was told to continue orbiting around the crash site. Hercules 326, with a para-rescue team aboard, was now on its way along with another unit. All three would be joined by Rescue Helicopter 307. Forty-year old Master Corporal Harvey Copeland gazed out Rescue 326, piloted by American Exchange Officer Captain Neil Toby, as it winged over the crash site.

"On the first passover it was quite easy to see the shelter. It was a big V. It just looked like a big black rock. He was standing in front waving both arms."

A 23-year veteran of the military, Copeland was quite confident the survivor was Marten Hartwell, but he was not positive.

"We weren't sure whether it was him, the boy, the nurse, or the other woman. I was very, very surprised and very excited that there was still someone alive. In my own mind, for some reason or other, I always thought there would be someone alive."

Copeland knew he would soon be making his 532nd jump. With him would be his partner on the flight, 30-year-old Al Williams. Williams, married and the father of six children, would be making only his second jump during an actual rescue operation.

The survivor, waiting below, could see two red streamers coming down from the sky. They had been released from the Herc, which by now was travelling at a speed of near 170 miles per hour, to provide the crew with a wind indication. As the survivor continued to gape skyward, the bundles dropped. He watched with relief as the two red and white parachutes opened and then a third yellow chute began floating towards him.

The first bundle contained a stove with some fuel, a six man tent and some sleeping bags. The second contained food, clothing and sleeping bags. The third was an accessory kit that contained food.

Harvey Copeland watched as they fell.

"The first bundle that didn't have food but was for heat and shelter landed about 12 feet away. He went out as though there was nothing wrong. All he did was cut the straps. The bundles weighed about 200 to 300 pounds and he was too weak and it was too heavy. I could see from the marks in the snow that he had carried it (some of the contents) to the tent right now. When I saw that, I figured there could have been other survivors but we didn't know."

The supplies had been dropped but there was now a new problem. Cloud was closing in and the lack of ceiling which had made it difficult during the drop would now have to be overcome for Copeland and Williams to jump. Al Williams was more at a disadvantage because of a lack of headsets in the aircraft. He didn't know what was happening until it happened; something which has since been resolved by authorities.

The Herc rumbled overhead at an altitude of 1,000 feet. Copeland had pre-determined with Captain Toby that the jump would be for a clearing east of the survivor. Copeland and Williams dropped.

"Al, stick with me!" he yelled.

Copeland knew the weather was deteriorating. He also knew that if he and Williams got half-a-mile apart they would never see each other.

"Al, I'm going for that clearing!"

The two rescuers drifted down about 100 feet apart.

"The work is just starting now," Harvey Copeland said to his partner when they landed.

They were about a half-mile from the survivor. If the ceiling had been 1,000 feet, Copeland estimates they would have landed right where the shelter was.

"We didn't anticipate the snow to be as deep as it was, but it was three feet of soft snow. We hit the ground at 20 to 1 (p.m.). I had the radio and Al had all the medical supplies for him and I if we needed them. Our main supplies were already at the crash site. In this case I knew where to go. We had flown over the clearing several times. We asked for a magnetic bearing. From the air we thought it was about a half-mile and that it would be about a half-hour walk."

As the long trek began, Rescue 307, a helicopter with a five man crew, was nearing the crash site.

Corporal Fred Doucette, a qualified loadmaster under training on his first search and rescue mission, learned there was a survivor.

The 26-year-old father of one, who joined the service after becoming fed-up working in a shoe factory, filled with excitement as he thought about the turn of events.

"We're going to save somebody. We've gotta get them out. I've gotta keep my composure and do my job."

Thinking back Doucette said, "I psyched myself into preparing for the worst; such as bodies being scattered all over the place but at the same time knew there was a job to be done."

Thirty-year-old Corporal Lance Roe, a technician who called himself a "flying mechanic", was ecstatic. He had been involved in two previous search and rescue missions and there had been no survivors in either.

"It's the first time I've ever been involved in picking up a survivor and my first thought was — thank God!"

Master Corporal Bob Bisson, the senior loadmaster aboard the chopper, had been involved in a number of search and rescue operations.

He said, "99 per cent of the time there aren't any survivors. At first I didn't know it was the aircraft we had been looking for. I just assumed it couldn't be Hartwell. Then when I learned it was the Beechcraft 18 and that there was one survivor, I was very curious as to who it was. Things went pretty quick after that."

Thirty-nine-year-old Major Austin Hayes was preparing to land Rescue 307. Beside him at the controls was Captain Gary McPhail. The 28-year-old McPhail had been involved in many previous searches, including operations in the North Atlantic and Labrador.

Even though conditions were far from ideal, he had complete confidence in the ability of the well experienced Major Hayes to bring in the helicopter safely. Hayes, a 21-year veteran of the services, had picked up about 50 people from various search and rescue operations on land and sea.

According to McPhail, "we were in a pretty tight spot with having to make an urgent landing with the trees and snow. There was also the risk of white-out conditions, where the chopper blades would whip up the snow, cutting visibility. Major Hayes flew over once, blew off some of the snow, and gave us a better idea of what we were landing in. He then set it down without any problem."

CRASH SITE — Deep snow blankets the scene. The lean-to at the right of the wreckage offered refuge.

THE WRECKAGE — Smashed aircraft parts and the makeshift shelter.

SURVIVAL TENT — It was made from sleeping bags, engine covers, stretchers and a blanket.

SILENT WITNESS — The interior of the tent bears silent witness to what had taken place.

5

"Welcome to the Camp of the Cannibal," were the words from Marten Hartwell as one of his rescuers approached.

It was shocking, but certainly no more so than the grisly scene that awaited those first into the area.

Master Corporal Bob Bisson was out of the copter and on his way through the deep snow. He knew there was at least one survivor but was still unsure about the others.

"He could see me coming," recalled the military man, "and he didn't shout nor did I."

The senior loadmaster was the first crew member to reach the survivor and would be alone with him for two to three minutes before the others arrived. The conversation was something he will never forget. Neither was the ghastly sight that confronted him.

"Hello Mr. Hartwell. How are ya?" asked Bisson.

"I'm fine", replied the haggard looking survivor.

"Have you had anything to eat from the rations?"

"Yes, but everything is frozen."

The conversation ended almost as quickly as it had begun. The rescuer, amazed at the physical condition and mental alertness of the filthy looking pilot, slowly moved his eyes from the matted and unclean beard. It was long and scraggly, the same as Hartwell's hair, but otherwise the pilot's general appearance was that of a man in remarkably good shape.

As he scanned the wilderness camp that had been this man's sequestered home for such a long time, Bisson spotted the wrappers that had been torn away from the raisin boxes and chocolate bars dropped from the Hercules rescue unit such a short time before. As his eyes shifted away from the discarded wrappings they suddenly became fixed on a hump near the opening of the makeshift shelter. Bisson at first refused to believe that what he was now looking at was what remained of what had been a human body. To him it appeared unreal, because if it was a corpse, it looked as though it had been butchered like an animal. He automatically assumed that it was a hind-quarter of a caribou or moose and it was only then, when the survivor broke the silence, that he realized the full horror of what had taken place.

"The others are all gone," said Hartwell, "I'm the only one left."

"If you had been six days earlier the boy would still be alive. The woman is over there by the tree. The boy is over there, and this is where Judy the nurse is, and this is where the rest of her is."

Bisson followed the survivor's pointing finger towards the tent.

"I assumed it was there. I noticed an axe leaning across the body. It was good and sharp. Then it hit me what had happened and I turned away. He told me all about it. I was shaking alright. It set me back a few paces."

The rescuer, stunned by the gruesome discovery, told Hartwell he would be right back. He then walked away to warn the others who were by now just a short distance away.

"It's an awful mess and a bad case of cannibalism," was the warning given Major Austin Hayes as he moved slowly through the deep snow towards the shelter. It was at this point that Hayes, an ace military man who does not wince easily, was greeted with the unforgettable words mouthed by Marten Hartwell.

"Welcome to the Camp of the Cannibal," shouted the survivor who at the same time was wolfing down peaches from one of the ration boxes.

"He was in extremely fine condition mentally, considering what he had been through," recalled Major Hayes, "he was very alert."

"His mental attitude was astounding. There was no hesitancy. He was completely wide open."

Corporal Fred Doucette, on his initial search and rescue mission, was not far behind the Major.

"I only saw the nurse," said Doucette, "it was terrible."

"I stood at the door of the tent and looked in. There wasn't much I could do. I left to help break a trail for the para-rescue guys."

The nauseating discovery spread like a disease. Captain Gary McPhail was there at about the same time as Doucette.

"I offered him a cigarette," stated McPhail, "he wondered whether he should take it and then Major Hayes offered him one and he accepted." The Captain, feeling sick to his stomach, fought back the urge to vomit and returned to the chopper.

The two para-rescue members, Harvey Copeland and Al Williams, were by this time nearing the survival tent. After trudging through the deep snow for about half-an-hour the sweat was rolling off their bodies. They were met by Lance Roe who had been breaking a trail for them. "The survivor is Hartwell," shouted Roe.

As they drew closer they could hear Hartwell frantically yelling, "Here! Here!"

"We're on our way!", yelled Copeland, "it's O.K.!"

"Boy, are we glad to find you alive!" said one of the military men.

"Not as glad as I am," replied Hartwell.

Within seconds Copeland reached the survivor.

Hartwell, on his knees in front of the shelter, bypassed the outstretched hand of the rescuer and grabbed him. There were no words during the brief and partial embrace but Copeland was fully aware of its meaning.

"Don't worry about a thing," he told Hartwell, "it's happened before."

The rescuer, who had made more than 530 parachute jumps and had been in para-rescue work for 17 years, was not merely making conversation. He had been in many survival camps and it would not be unreasonable nor necessarily inaccurate to think that he had seen evidence of cannibalism prior to this — even though it had never been made public.

The words that Marten Hartwell used to respond to Copeland are hazy, although he did make it clear how he felt.

According to one of his rescuers, "he replied in a way that he didn't want the world to know. He was ashamed. I think he'd have sooner stayed there if he knew the world would know. He wanted to keep it a secret. There was no crying or anything like that. That's why his mental attitude was so good."

Earlier, Hartwell left the impression that there was no shame in what had taken place. He appeared more relieved that he was going to be picked up and even expressed concern that certain evidence not be disturbed.

He became excited when one of the military men retrieved the Dart II emergency locater transmitter to shut it off. He said he wanted it because it saved his life, but he cautioned the rescuer not to touch it, because, "the aerial is broken."

The crash area presented a macabre sight. To the right of a big tree near the shelter was the Inuit woman. Wearing a blue nightgown, she had been covered by a sheet that was topped by newly fallen snow. The body of David Kootook was in front of the tree and beyond this were the dismembered remains of nurse, Judy Hill. She had been dragged in front of the tent and her truncated torso remained within hand's reach of the shelter. The single headed axe was leaning against her body after having been used to chop her limbs.

"One of the nurses legs was in two pieces," recalled one of the rescuers. "Both had been severed in sort of a V at the crotch."

"One leg was all together but the other had been chopped at the knee," related the serviceman. "Her light blue panties were still on and so were her blue socks."

Inside the tent, where the axe had by now been placed by one of the rescuers, was the ration box.

There were several plastic bags containing flesh from the body of nurse Hill. According to one of the rescuers, Hartwell "consumed quite a bit," but there still remained an estimated 10 pounds of flesh inside the box, some of it just chips and bits of the hacked nurse's remains.

It looked as though the survivor had set a daily ration system.

"Hartwell is the sole survivor," radioed Major Austin Hayes to search headquarters.

He then asked permission to bring everything out from the death camp but was told, "No! Just bring Hartwell out."

The rescuers realized it was now definitely a police matter.

Marten Hartwell was not given any medical treatment at the scene.

"He was down there for 32 days," explained Harvey Copeland. "He told us about his smashed ankles, nose, and hand and there's no way we would attempt to do too much. It would just complicate things for complete treatment that was only a short time away. We tried to comfort him and keep him warm."

"Mentally and physically he was in damn good shape," remembered one member of the search team. "He was in better shape than I was in."

Another serviceman disagreed saying, "he seemed to be in another world. It sort of scared me. I thought, is this guy going to crack up on me or what?"

Hartwell, when told he would have to go to the hospital, said he wished he did not have to.

"I'd go out and celebrate", he said, "it's my birthday."

He later explained, "it's not really my birthday, but as far as I'm concerned I'm going to celebrate it as a birthday ... this is day one."

The 'Alive' pilot's right ankle was in bad shape. It was swollen and deformed. His one leg was bent like a banana and yet in spite of the throbbing pain he wanted to walk to the waiting helicopter. He was persuaded not to and was placed in a sleeping bag and then carried out by stretcher to the waiting machine. The survivor was placed on his stomach because he wanted to talk. He had a lot to say including a demand that the letters he had written be brought out with him. He was told they would be brought out later.

"No! I want it (the bag of letters) to come out now", insisted Hartwell. "Those are the personal effects of everybody."

His demand was not met and the letters would later be turned over to the Royal Canadian Mounted Police.

Aboard the chopper, Hartwell feverishly consumed pears, raisins and a Hershey chocolate bar.

He talked virtually non-stop and smoked incessantly throughout the nearly two hour helicopter trip to Yellowknife.

He described his survival from day-one to day-32. He told of making a diary, having fires everyday, and running out of liquid fuel (gasoline) after the 15th day. He said the 28th day was the last time he had a fire, having used kindling up until that time. Fire didn't seem that important to him. He said he ate the meat from the nurse's body, raw, and claimed he could have lasted another month.

His rescuers disagreed.

Harvey Copeland, an expert on survival thought, "he could have lasted only another week regardless of the food supply because of the moisture that gets in the sleeping bags. With the condensation he couldn't have lasted more than a week."

When Marten Hartwell made the assertion about living another month, perhaps he was only thinking of food. He said he thought of the others. He knew where the bodies were but to prepare them to eat would be difficult. He was not too sure where he would begin with the remaining frozen cadavers. The survivor continued to ramble on. He told of putting the meat in his sleeping bag and warming it with body heat to thaw it out. He then ate the chunks of flesh raw. He talked about it the same way as if he had gotten a rabbit.

Hartwell chain-smoked throughout the helicopter medical

evacuation. He singed his hair. He also complained. He was upset about the internal tanks in the helicopter because together with the supplies it made a tight spot for him. Once he was settled in he was alright. He talked about his days in Germany and how bad he felt about the crash. He asked his rescuers if they knew Susan Haley and was told that both she and her mother were waiting in Yellowknife. He said he found that interesting because he had been using cards to tell his future and they told him that two women would meet him. He was surprised, glad to know his girlfriend had not given up, and repeated, "today is my birthday — this is day one."

Hartwell repeatedly asked for reassurance that what had taken place at the camp would not be made public. He thought there was a law against it, and he was worried about the legal ramifications.

He also disclosed that he normally did not eat meat, "you won't believe it but I'm a vegetarian and look at what's happened to me."

Harvey Copeland replied, "you're still alive, you've gotta live, so don't worry about it. When you're up against it you've just got to live."

Hartwell continued to tell of his past. He said that Susan was his girlfriend and that they had lived together for eight months at Fort Norman. He also mentioned that he had a son (20-year-old Peer), a wife, and a mother-in-law and left the distinct impression that he didn't get along with his mother-in-law. He married in 1948 and his son had been born four years later.

Rescue 307 landed at Yellowknife. It was 3:20 p.m. Marten Hartwell was loaded into a waiting ambulance. The news media had been alerted nearly two hours earlier that there had been one survivor. It was not revealed, however, who that person was. Officials, in an attempt to withhold the information until relatives of the dead could be notified, made arrangements to have the helicopter land in the middle of the airfield. A news photographer managed to get close enough though, and the picture he captured was that of Marten Hartwell. The former German airforce pilot was the lone survivor. The others had perished.

The pilot was rushed to hospital. He had survived a trial that would have claimed the lives of most. He had suffered fractures to both ankles and one knee. The rations aboard the death plane had run out. There had been heavy snow. Temperatures at one time plummeted to 41 degrees below zero and with winds reaching 24 miles an hour, the wind chill factor at one time had dropped temperatures to 60-below Fahrenheit. Despite the 32-day tragic drama in the Arctic wilds, Hartwell was described by Armed Forces doctor Warren Edward Harrison, as, "quite mentally alert and in good spirits."

"Physically he appeared to have suffered considerably, but was still in quite good shape," said Dr. Harrison, noting that the survivor was putrid, having not been out of his clothes since his hell on earth began.

"He weighed 140 pounds I believe at the time," said the doctor. "Hartwell stated he had weighed approximately 170 pounds before the accident. I had never seen the patient before so I had no idea."

The doctor credited exceptionally warm clothing — a parka, two or three pairs of overalls, a heavy set of underwear and a thick vest — for protecting Hartwell from the harsh elements.

X-rays confirmed that the survivor had a broken left knee and two broken ankles. The injuries meant that he would have been unable to walk during his lonely vigil.

From his hospital bed he told that nurse Judy Hill died in the crash, the pregnant woman with labor complications a few days later, and the boy 23 days after the plane had slammed into the hillside.

He was quoted as saying that the youth died shortly after a plane passed almost directly overhead, but didn't spot them, even though they had a fire burning. The pilot told an official with his company, Gateway Aviation Limited, that the plane worked perfectly but for some unexplained reason the radio beacon at Contwoyto Lake was missed. He said he then started to go off course but could still pick up signals from Fort Franklin and Fort Reliance. The plane, according to Hartwell, was flying at about 2,500 feet because of a low ceiling when he turned on his cockpit light and pulled out maps to determine his position. He crashed shortly afterwards into a 2,000 foot hill.

Hartwell told of the freezing, the hunger, and the suffering. Restricted to a diet of baby food when first taken to hospital he related how he had survived by eating lichens and dextrose, and getting water by munching snow. The story differed from what had been seen and heard at the crash location by rescuers, but what was related from the hospital bed went unchallenged. Newspapers around the world headlined stories telling of the miraculous survival of one man against unbelievable odds. Reporters from all over Canada, the United States and Europe made attempts to purchase the exclusive rights to the story that they believed only Hartwell could tell. A veil of secrecy had been placed over all of those directly involved in the rescue which was now under full investigation by the RCMP.

Hartwell had already received numerous assurances that his secret would be kept, and as he lay in the hospital bed with his girlfriend Susan Haley nearby, he pondered what to do. He had told his much younger female companion what he had done to live.

She knew and had not rejected him. Moreover, this young woman who had criticized the search and rescue operation and would later take exception to the persistence of the news media, would soon be discussing the monetary value of her boyfriend's story.

One of the Armed Forces rescuers entered the hospital. Hartwell had asked him to come up and see him so he could thank him in a better way. He entered the room and was embraced momentarily by Susan Haley.

"Don't worry about it she knows," said Hartwell from his bed.

They talked about a number of things.

Hartwell asked, "what did you do with the bag?"

The bag of letters was already in the possession of the RCMP, he was told.

Hartwell seemed more mentally alert than before. He said he was going to sell his story. He had offers from the German press, the English press and from the news media in the United States. He had not accepted any of the offers and asked what he should do.

The rescuer told him, "there's only one person who can decide that and that's you — so don't ask me."

Hartwell remained silent.

The military man waited a few minutes and then departed. As he walked out of the room he thought back to the numerous times Hartwell had asked that the story be kept quiet. Those wishes were being respected and now he was willing to tell the story for money.

The soldier felt hurt, "I didn't think he'd think of money but when I got to the hospital it was definitely dollars and cents."

Marten Hartwell was also visited by two members of the Royal Canadian Mounted Police. Corporal Robert Anderson and Constable Gerald Tilley identified themselves. They were aware of a possible violation of Section 178 of the Criminal Code (dealing with the commission of an indignity to a dead human body or human remains), but they did not raise the matter.

Hartwell talked on his own, in truth it is one of the first things he told the investigating officers.

"I have something I want to tell you," he said, and went on to explain that he had been forced to consume human flesh in order to survive.

The information was jotted down by the policemen to be used later in court if it was necessary.

Both members remained in the hospital room for approximately 20 minutes. No attempt was made to obtain a formal statement because plans were underway to move Hartwell to a hospital in Edmonton.

Hartwell was advised by police to "remain silent for your own good" and "seek legal advice."

The lawyer retained by Marten Hartwell was Brian Purdy. He was brought in to deal with the news media. The Yellowknife lawyer was quoted as saying, "every time he opens his mouth another $1,000 goes down the drain."

Purdy later explained, "he was literally besieged by the news media and I was trying to explain his position that he had offers for his story. I told them, you're asking him in effect to throw $25,000 down the drain."

Because the doctors decided that Hartwell would be moved to Edmonton for hospital treatment, Purdy telephoned lawyer James Creighton (Red) Cavanagh. He had known the 56-year-old Edmonton lawyer from a previous case and called to ask if he would take over once Hartwell was moved from Yellowknife.

"Purdy didn't know anything about the cannibalism," according to Cavanagh.

It was after this that the pilot said that when the story would be sold the proceeds would be shared with the relatives of the victims.

THE ARRIVAL—
The survivor
crawls from an
aircraft on arrival
in Edmonton.

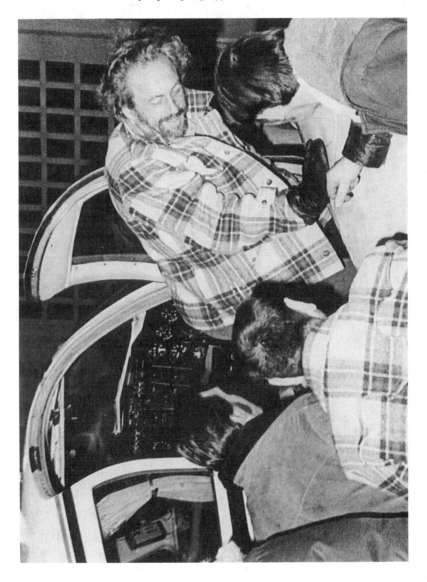

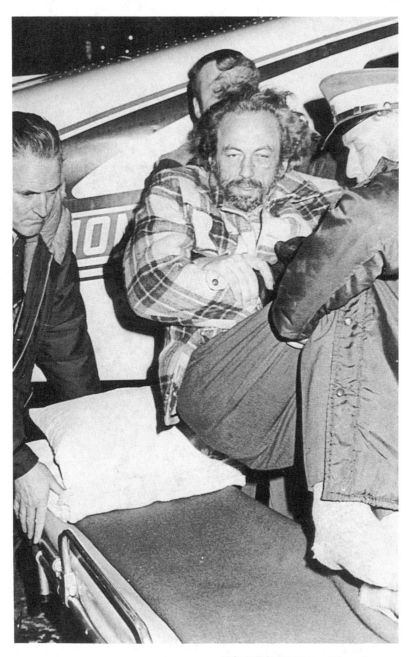

TO HOSPITAL — Placed on a
stretcher he was rushed away
for medical treatment.

6

The bones were found near the shelter under a seat from the smashed Beechcraft. The ration box with its plastic bags of flesh remained. So did the slashed remains of the nurse, the other bodies and the sick feeling that permeated those who had been there before. It was two days after the initial rescue that some of the Armed Forces personnel were back to again glimpse the terror that had taken place. This time they were accompanied by the police. Constable Ron Kingdon, the key investigating officer, was ordering the area dug up. It was necessary to ensure that everything of consequence was brought out and it was only after this that the grim task of preparing the victims for removal got underway.

According to one of the rescuers, all of the remains of Judy Hill were not located.

"There was a fair amount in the ration box," he recalled. "There were a lot of chips. There were no big pieces. There were slivers and bits and pieces near the body. They never got it all out. It snowed, and sure they dug up the area, but they never got everything out."

Another member of the rescue team, who said Hartwell told him that the boy helped him drag the nurse's body within hands reach of the tent continued, "there was only one bone missing and that was one of the thigh bones. Both of them were there the first day but when we went back it wasn't there. It has never been found. Whether someone chucked it in the snow, I don't know, but that's probably what happened."

Four body bags were used to remove what had to be taken from the crash scene. One for the Inuit woman. One for the emaciated body of David Kootook. Another for the upper portion of nurse Judy Hill and her flesh and bone that had been lopped off and another for personal belongings that had been rounded up by the searchers.

The body bags, or pouches, were loaded onto the helicopter for the journey to Yellowknife.

"It was the worst thing any of the guys had seen," recalled one of the investigators, "and there's guys with a lot of experience who witnessed it."

There were an estimated 40 persons in the hanger at Yellowknife when the chopper was emptied. They included members of the military, the RCMP and an inquest jury.

Regardless of the number of people now aware of what had taken place and those who knew for two days and didn't speak of the abnormal food supply, the silence would continue. The truth would remain covered up at least as far as the general public was concerned because they were dependent on the news media that was being stifled. The case had become shrouded in a cloak of concealment.

Forty-one-year-old RCMP Inspector Tom Venner was about to go to bed. It was 11:30 p.m., Monday, December 11th. The telephone rang. On the other end was Inspector Hugh Feagan. The Officer Commanding, Yellowknife Sub-Division, was requesting assistance. He explained that Constable Ron Kingdon was accompanying the bodies of the three victims into Edmonton. Kingdon would be identifying them for the purpose of the autopsy and would require help from a local member who was familiar with the pathologists and the facilities.

Inspector Venner said that he would arrange for a member of the homicide detail to work closely with Kingdon and give him all the help he required.

Inspector Feagan continued, "there's another complication with this file in that Hartwell has admitted the consumption of human flesh."

Inspector Feagan explained that because Hartwell was being transferred from Yellowknife, there had not been sufficient time to obtain a written statement. He asked that Inspector Venner assist Constable Kingdon in obtaining a 'warned written statement'; a document taken from him after he had been given the standard police warning and made well aware that there were some criminal charges which possibly could attend to what had taken place.

Inspector Feagan hung up. He went back to planning the investigation. Inspector Venner again picked up his telephone and called an Edmonton hotel where he left a message for Constable Kingdon.

The call was returned within about half-an-hour and arrangements were made for a meeting at the RCMP headquarters the next morning.

The three deceased were now at the General hospital in Edmonton. They had been flown in under the cover of darkness. The plane landed at the city's downtown Industrial Airport. The sealed pouches were removed and placed in an ambulance to be transported to the morgue. The pouches never left the sight of Constable Kingdon and once they arrived at the hospital they were placed in a locked room awaiting pathological studies. Technicians and others involved in the examination were sworn to secrecy. Back at Yellowknife, Coroner Walter England and the RCMP had cordoned off an area taking in a 25-mile radius of the crash zone.

The next morning Inspector Venner reported to his superior, Superintendent W.G. Pritchard. He asked for a member of the homicide detail to be made available to assist in the investigation. Constable Bob Preston was assigned the job.

Constable Kingdon arrived at Inspector Venner's office at the arranged time of 9 a.m. and the two police officers, along with Bob Preston, reviewed everything that was known from the time the aircraft was discovered. Inspector Venner then made arrangements with an official of the Misericordia hospital so he could interview Marten Hartwell. The other two investigators went over to the General hospital where they would discuss with pathologist, Dr. Laurier Boutin, plans for the autopsies.

Red Cavanagh had a dinner appointment the night before. He had made arrangements to have a member of the same law firm, Roy Henning, meet Hartwell at the airport upon his arrival. The next morning neither lawyer knew anything about the consumption of human flesh.

Cavanagh entered the hospital room where he would meet his new client for the first time.

He recalled, "he was on the thin side, he had whiskers and his hair was kind of wild. He had a bit of an accent."

The lawyer had only been in Hartwell's room for a few minutes when a hospital official went up and advised him that an RCMP officer was waiting downstairs.

Inspector Venner then went up and greeted Red Cavanagh, whom he had known for years, outside the survivor's room. They spoke briefly and then entered a room off the hallway where Inspector Venner explained that he was there to conduct an interview with Hartwell.

"What about?" asked the lawyer.

He was told that the interview was necessary because of the possibility of criminal negligence in connection with the aircraft accident. The police wanted the details of the mercy flight. Why and under what circumstances and whether Hartwell was certified to take the flight.

"Well, my advice will be to my client at the moment not to say anything to the police at this time," said the Edmonton lawyer. "I haven't had a chance to fully discuss it with him."

Venner then asked, "has your client discussed any other aspect of this that might cause him some difficulties?"

"What do you mean?" replied Cavanagh.

Venner went on, "there is another section of the Criminal Code which may have been violated."

He then referred the lawyer to section 178 which he had looked up earlier that morning.

DEAD BODY

178 Everyone Who

(a) Neglects without lawful excuse to perform any duty that is imposed upon him by law or that he undertakes with reference to the burial of a dead human body or human remains;

(b) Improperly or indecently interferes with or offers any indignity to a dead human body or human remains whether buried or not

Is guilty of an indictable offence and liable to imprisonment for five years.

Venner was the first to speak, "for your information there's been an admission made by Hartwell up there to two of our members that he did consume human flesh in an effort to survive."

Cavanagh was astonished. This was the first he had heard of what had taken place. Both men briefly discussed the wording of the Criminal Code section and whether it would apply under the circumstances.

Cavanagh then said, "well, my advice to my client now more than ever is that he should not say anything to the police at this time, certainly until I have had a chance to discuss this aspect with him thoroughly because he hasn't informed me of this and it's a genuine surprise to me at this time."

Venner persisted, "for the purposes of my report on the investigation, it makes a difference to me whether this declining to say anything to the police at this time comes from your client or comes from his lawyer. I would like to ask him, and if he declines to talk to the police at this time, well that's fine. I'll be warning him and telling him the reason for being here is in very general terms."

"Fine," said Cavanagh, "I'll go and tell him."

Within about two minutes the lawyer emerged and motioned

Inspector Venner into the room. Hartwell was sitting up in bed. His constant companion, Susan Haley, was in the room along with Doug Rae, the man who hired him at Gateway Aviation. Inspector Venner was introduced by lawyer Cavanagh. Hartwell, dressed in a hospital gown, still had quite a growth of beard. He seemed alert and in good health.

Inspector Venner produced his RCMP identification.

"I have been asked by our Yellowknife headquarters to interview you concerning all the details of your personal history, the record of your employment, the mercy flight, the crash itself, the deaths of the three other persons, and your survival."

"Why?" demanded Hartwell.

Venner replied, "there are a lot of things that our members haven't had time to clear up yet due to the lack of opportunity to interview you in Yellowknife."

He also told the survivor that he had spoken with Mr. Cavanagh and that he understood his lawyer's advice was that he should not say anything to the police at this time.

Hartwell then replied, "I have already talked to the police in Yellowknife and they have access to letters which I had written. I cannot see why any more details than were contained in those letters are necessary."

The RCMP Inspector told him that he was aware of the content of the conversation with the police in Yellowknife. He told him that as a result of that discussion any interview that took place now would only be conducted after he had been advised of certain rights.

"Including the fact that you do not have to talk to me at all," the Inspector concluded.

Hartwell stated, "in that case I will have to say that I have no comment to make."

The Mountie remained in the room for only a short time afterwards. He spoke very briefly with Hartwell about the pilot's condition and during the entire visit noted how remarkably placid was this man who had just come through such misery.

"He certainly wasn't upset or emotionally distraught or anything like that. He was very composed and handled himself very well. He spoke very clearly."

Inspector Venner returned to the RCMP headquarters where he was told that the bodies were so thoroughly frozen that it would take at least two or three days before the autopsies could be performed. An appointment was then made with officials of the RCMP crime detection laboratory. They were briefed on the situation and asked for guidance on the type of exhibits that would be necessary.

Inspector Venner explained, "there was human flesh found in the tent up at the crash site. In order for the investigation to be thorough and complete we had to determine which body that human flesh came from. There was visible evidence to support this, but we not only had to satisfy ourselves that it came from a certain body, but also that it didn't come from another body."

Constables Ron Kingdon and Bob Preston were assigned the job of finding out more about Marten Hartwell. It was learned his legal name was Leopold Herrmann and he had started proceedings to change it to Marten Hartwell. He had not finalized the legal procedure. There were difficulties in determining how, when, and under what circumstances he had come to Canada, and initially there were problems in finding a record of his entry into Canada. 'G' Division, which is the North for the RCMP, has its headquarters in Ottawa and much of the work ferreting out background information on Hartwell was being carried out there. It was a team effort that involved assistance from many detachments. It would be necessary to talk with all of Hartwell's employers in an effort to gain as much information about him as possible. It would also be necessary to interview individuals who could provide valuable information but were now out of the Arctic region. Hartwell had no criminal record in Canada.

A list of rations aboard the death plane was obtained by the RCMP. An accounting that the investigators have satisfied themselves is correct. It contained:

- six seven-ounce cans of corned beef
- four packages of dehydrated chicken noodle soup
- twelve oxo cubes
- one 12-ounce package of rice
- one package of powdered potatoes (about the equivalent of five to six fairly large sized potatoes).
- An unspecified number of glucose pills (perhaps around 40).
- twelve small packages of raisins (packages that sold for about five cents).

The survival kit was also supposed to contain two pounds of pilot biscuits but they were not in the ration box.

Dr. Laurier Boutin, 38, knew that he would be performing the autopsies on the three plane crash victims. He had heard about the discovery on the news.

"I was sort of half hoping that they wouldn't be sent here," said Dr. Boutin, "but because of the connection with an aircraft accident they were automatically brought here."

The evening the bodies were flown in, the general pathologist was notified by Dr. J.J. Lapinski, the Medical Director of the General hospital.

"He was a bit surprised by these three bodies being brought in by the RCMP," recalled Dr. Boutin, "it was because of the security aspect."

The corpses were brought in on the evening of December 11th, but because they were frozen, the autopsies could not be performed until the 14th. They were left to thaw under normal room temperature in the hospital's main morgue.

Dr. Boutin did not know prior to viewing the bodies that one of them had been mutilated. He was faced with the remains of a young boy who was no more than skin and bone — too thin to still be breathing — a pregnant woman, and a young woman who had been dissevered with an axe and partially eaten.

"It was a shock, but something that we are somewhat trained to be ready for," said the doctor, "also, to me it explained the situation."

"From what you found in the boy's stomach, when was the last time that he would have eaten according to what you can figure?" he was later questioned by a reporter.

"I think according to what I found in his bowels, quite possibly the last time he had eaten was maybe 12 hours or more before, and could be a few days," replied the doctor.

"And there is no way from what you can determine in your lab tests whether or not he would have had half of the amount of food?" asked the newsman. "You know there was a list of food on the plane? Could you determine that?"

"No, I don't think I could; only indirectly like anybody, I think, could postulate that. Let's say he ate half of it and he was active as opposed to Mr. Hartwell who had broken bones and couldn't walk. There was also waist deep snow. If you want to travel any distance in that type of snow you've got to expend an awful lot of energy. If he ate half of it, in a young kid whose metabolism is a little faster than an older person, certainly he would use it up a lot faster. Also, the type of food that he ate, aside from that vegetable food, I doubt would give him that much energy and calorie intake. In other words, I have no reason from my examination to state that he did not get his share, but your guess is just as good as mine as far as that goes."

Dr. Laurier Boutin had performed about 300 autopsies. His final report in connection with the Marten Hartwell plane crash would not be finalized until weeks later.

December 14th. The autopsies were being performed and at almost the same time Inspector Tom Venner was again meeting with lawyer Red Cavanagh. Both men discussed the feasibility of Marten Hartwell providing a full 'warned statement' to the authorities. The question of what really had taken place at the crash site was becoming coffee shop conversation.

"Because of the stories that are growing every day and with so obviously many of them inaccurate," stated Inspector Venner, "it seems to me that your client's position would best be served by giving a full accurate statement to the police."

"Before I give any further advice to my client," said Red

Cavanagh, "I'm interested in knowing whether or not there will be any prosecutions under section 178 of the Code?"

"I'll consult with 'G' Division as to what their views are," answered Inspector Venner.

He returned to his office, telephoned Ottawa, and was told, "we have not been able to come to any final conclusion — we are in no position to say whether there will or will not be criminal charges under section 178."

The information was relayed to Red Cavanagh who again advised his client not to say anything to the police. Part of that recommendation was based on Hartwell's medical condition. He had been operated on twice within the preceding few weeks.

In the intervening period, the investigation centred in Yellowknife. Additional evidence was being gathered and witnesses were being readied for the inquest. Information was being forwarded to the North from Edmonton — vital data that became known following pathological studies on the victims.

"We were unable from the autopsy report and the lab analysis to conclude that there had been any withholding of food from the boy. We were satisfied that his death had come about by starvation and there is nothing inconsistent with this in the lab reports or in the autopsy reports themselves," Inspector Venner stated. "There was nothing which was inconsistent with death by starvation and the probable sharing of what rations we knew to be on board that aircraft."

The Inspector knew, however, that determining exactly how much the boy had eaten was not that precise a science.

"I don't think they can take a look at stomach contents and everything and say this boy had so many pounds of food to eat in so many days. It just can't be done."

During the next month there was communication on an average of about once a week between Inspector Venner and lawyer Cavanagh.

It was also during this time that the Federal Justice Department appointed lawyer William Trainor to handle the case on behalf of the Crown.

He arrived in Edmonton in mid-January and began interviewing all available witnesses.

He also held talks along with Inspector Venner in the office of lawyer Cavanagh. They revolved around the possibility of charges being laid in connection with criminal negligence and section 178 of the Code. Lawyer Cavanagh was not given any commitment that the possibility of charges being laid had been ruled out.

"For one thing it's a perfectly legitimate function of a coroner's jury to direct that charges be laid, and it's being rather presumptuous for instance on the part of an agent of the Minister of Justice to say there will be no charges until after a jury has given its views," Inspector Venner stated. He continued, "that's not to say that because a jury says there should be criminal charges that there would be criminal charges but it would, as I say, be presumptuous for somebody to say there won't be until they have at least heard the views of the coroner's jury."

It was at this meeting that Inspector Venner and lawyer Trainor were allowed to read a 15-page statement dictated by Marten Hartwell (he could not write because of injuries to his hand) and written by Susan Haley.

"It only dealt with the crash and up to the point where David Kootook had died and Marten Hartwell was right out of food. Nothing left to eat at all," according to Inspector Venner. He added, "on reading it I informed Mr. Cavanagh that this was the type of statement that I had in mind, but the one I would be asking for would be more complete. It would cover matters ahead of that, right up to the point when he was first approached about taking the mercy flight, and matters subsequent to that. About how he survived, and was there any consumption of human flesh, to what degree and so forth."

The continual contact between Inspector Venner and lawyer Cavanagh kept up during the following weeks. It was decided nearly a month later that Marten Hartwell would meet with the Inspector and provide a statement. The meeting was set for February 14th.

At 2 o'clock that afternoon Inspector Venner was handed a 24-page copy of a handwritten document. He then 'warned' Marten Hartwell.

"There are matters that we have to discuss first and I want you to be sure of your rights. There is still the possibility of criminal charges being laid in the area of criminal negligence and also in relation to section 178 of the Criminal Code. It has to do with offering an indignity to a dead body."

"I fully understand that," confirmed the pilot.

Inspector Venner continued, "Marten Hartwell, you need not say anything, you have nothing to hope from any promise or favor, and nothing to fear from any threat whether or not you say anything. Anything you do say may be used as evidence. Do you fully understand this?"

Hartwell acknowledged that he understood.

Inspector Venner, referring to the document, continued, "are you saying that this is an accurate accounting of your activities as dictated by you to Miss Haley and as written by her?"

"Yes, although I want to make a change at the top of page 11 of that statement," replied Hartwell.

The words then deleted were, "from the headphones." He explained that the way they were written in, left the wrong impression. It indicated that he had been knocked out or that injuries had been caused to his head by the headphones in the crash.

Hartwell found it significant enough to delete the words because he wanted it understood that the headphones had become twisted sideways and when he hit the dashboard he thought it must have been the headphones that caused the bruises and cuts on his nose.

"If this is the only correction you want to make, then would you sign your initials here?" asked the RCMP inspector.

Marten Hartwell signed his name.

Inspector Venner told him, "I want to read the statement thoroughly, and after that there may be some questions I may want to ask in clarification of matters raised in the statement."

He proceeded to the kitchen table and began poring through the information, alone. The others; Hartwell, his girlfriend, and lawyer Cavanagh remained in the living room. About 30 minutes later, Inspector Venner had completed his reading.

He then told Hartwell, "I want to go over it and read it aloud with you at my elbow. Following that, I'll ask you to acknowledge that it's your statement and ask that you sign it."

"I'll sign it now as being an accurate statement," said Hartwell, who proceeded to initial every page and place his signature on the final sheet.

The two of them sat down with Lawyer Cavanagh at the kitchen table and Inspector Venner began reading it word for word.

"If there's anything you know that's in here that doesn't sound right," he said, "whether you think it could be worded better or is inaccurate, please speak up and we'll change it."

As they went along, clarification was sought on numerous points. It resulted in an additional 13 pages of handwritten notes being taken.

Marten Hartwell seemed to know exactly what he wanted to say. He wanted to tell the story. He wanted to make sure that it was very clear to Inspector Venner exactly what his position was. It became an emotional confrontation. The survivor was shown five photographs and asked to identify them. He was also questioned about the consumption of human flesh. He did not break down but it showed that he was extremely distressed. It brought back the horror of the madness that made him decide. His voice wavered. The excruciating, pained memories were mirrored in his face.

The document was then signed and initialed by both Hartwell and Inspector Venner. The ordeal had taken three hours and yet Hartwell did not appear overly relieved. Indeed, there was some relief detected in that it was over and done with, but it was not great enough to reveal whether it was because the statement had been given or merely because it was a long afternoon for everyone.

It was 5 p.m. Inspector Venner would relay the new development to 'G' Division headquarters in Ottawa. He would also advise, that in his opinion, Marten Hartwell would not be attending the inquest in Yellowknife. The RCMP now had the statement that had taken so long to obtain. Prior to leaving the apartment occupied by Hartwell and his girlfriend, lawyer Cavanagh called his office. He made arrangements for someone to go down to the florists and pick up some flowers that he had ordered for his wife. The meeting in the survivor's apartment had taken longer than anticipated and the florist shop would be closed by the time he got back to the office through rush-hour traffic. It was February 14th. Saint Valentine's Day.

7

Despite Marten Hartwell having now made his statement to the police, there was no public release of its contents to the news media. It had been obtained following great concern expressed by officials over the preposterous number of unsubstantiated rumors that began circulating and growing to incredulous proportions.

Rumors such as:

The nurses breasts had been cut off and placed in plastic bags.

The boy, in the care and control of an experienced, life hardened adult, had worked to death. It was true that he was at the beck and command of the pilot, an imposing, authoritative figure. It was also true that the Spence Bay youth was naive and afraid. He also respected his elders. It was a strong part of the Inuit culture.

He had not had his share of the rations.

The nurse's body was not the only one that was maimed.

Her's was not the only flesh that had been eaten.

The plane wasn't found until after the boy's death because then the complete truth of the terror and debauchery would never be known.

They were all rumors, but as they passed from the lips of one person to the ears of another, they grew in magnitude. The gossip became more savage and barbaric. It was becoming increasingly vicious. It would not stop.

The RCMP had adopted an attitude of replying "no comment" to any news media inquiries.

"No comment," they said, when questioned about the rumor that a substantial portion of flesh had been missing from the nurse's body.

"No comment," they replied in response to the fabrication about her breasts.

They had been put under strict orders of secrecy and they were admittedly in a difficult position. Unfortunately, the rumors; however ludicrous, were responded to by saying "no comment." Consequently, they were not squelched.

They continued and were later to develop into a series of indecent jokes. Many began prior to the inquest and still more were circulating afterwards.

The so-called humor, included:

Have you heard that Gateway Aviation has a new survival kit?

No, what does it contain?

A meat cleaver and a knife and fork.

Have you heard that the Ministry of Transport has given Hartwell his pilot's license back?

No.

Yeh, but there's one stipulation.

What's that?

He's gotta take his teeth out before he boards the aircraft.

Have you heard that Marten Hartwell wrote a manuscript but it was rejected?

No, why?

Because it was too short for a novel and too long for a menu.

It was repugnant. Yet — it persisted.

The RCMP continued to withhold comment. There were two reasons.

As one investigating officer said, "when a Coroner says information won't be released, well then it won't be released by the police anyway. That was one reason. The other was that our investigation was simply too incomplete. We just didn't have enough information and it's not our policy to release piecemeal little bits or part of an investigation."

On January 8th, more than five weeks before the RCMP had obtained an official statement from Hartwell, CHQT radio in Edmonton broadcast a news bulletin reporting that the body of the nurse had a substantial amount of flesh removed from its lower portion and that packages believed to contain human remains were obtained from the crash location.

In a following broadcast, the station reported, "pilot Hartwell admitted cannibalism to more than one person. He spoke quite freely about it for the first couple of days and the information is on record."

The broadcasts were the culmination of countless, continuous attempts to uncover shreds of information that would piece the full story together. It began in a snowy, parking lot when I expressed disbelief to a patrolling police officer that Hartwell survived by normal circumstances and was told, "Peter, check it out." Many of those involved in the investigation wanted to talk as they had been shocked at what they knew and at the misleading news the world was being given. They wanted to talk but they could not for fear of losing their jobs. Finally, after many days of trying to get the information out of everyone I could think of, one of many officials who did not want the truth suppressed, confirmed, "cannibalism did take place — he ate the nurse." I said, "that's fine but if we go to air with the story there has to be proof or we'll be sued for everything we own — how can you prove that was how he survived?" The reply, considering the source, was all that was needed. "It's easy", I was told, "we knew what she weighed when she got on the plane and we know what she weighs now."

Prior to the broadcast, the story was read to lawyer Red Cavanagh. He was asked if he had any comment and he answered, "No." Afterwards, the lawyer confirmed something that I already believed — if the story was erroneous then as a member of the court he would have an obligation to point out the mistake. Otherwise, if it was wrong and he did not say anything, it would have been impossible for him to later come back and successfully sue for damages on behalf of his client.

The two CHQT reports were chased by another Edmonton radio station, CHED. It reported in an editorial commentary to thousands of listeners that David Kootook admitted that his food supply consisted of human flesh. The station claimed it had been "told" the boy had left such a message, written in the snow, at the encampment.

An official involved in the investigation quickly dismissed the report, describing it as, "sad and wrong." He termed it, "imaginary and dangerous" and emphasized that the boy would be alive if his food supply had consisted of anything abnormal. He called the teenager a hero.

The CHED report was inaccurate and severely damaging to the memory of the youth. It also strained the credibility of one of the city's most popular radio stations.

Other than correcting the false broadcast, the RCMP continued to withold information. The mass circulation Observer newspaper in London, England then published a front-page report quoting the CHQT story. It was several weeks after the initial January 8th account that the Toronto Sun became the first newspaper in Canada to reveal the scope of what had taken place in the frozen Arctic. The publication date was February 26th, the day that the inquest was finally scheduled to get underway.

The reaction was the same as that received following the radio broadcasts nearly two months earlier. The story was dismissed as 'ridiculous' by many news gathering agencies. They said it was way off course, extremely dangerous and would lead to libel action. It was now time to either prove or disprove the reports which were criticized, termed outrageous, and questioned by those who refused to believe.

Reporters from around the world were descending on Yellowknife. The inquest would begin in a matter of hours.

8

The small, snowladen community provided a melancholy backdrop as the astonishing saga of the crashed Beechcraft moved into its inquiry stage. The inquest, under the direction of Coroner Walter Vernon England, convened officially in a Yellowknife aircraft hangar on December 11th. Once the victims had been identified, the inquest adjourned and was later tentatively scheduled to re-open February 19th. Another one week delay was then announced by Coroner England who said it was because of the unavailability of a witness who was holidaying outside the country.

Three different investigations and four government agencies were involved in the intervening probe. In addition to the Coroner's inquest and the separate RCMP investigation for police purposes, the Ministry of Transport, Territorial Government (GNWT), and Federal Justice Department were all involved in gathering central information.

A Trans-Atlantic spectrum of the world press was gathering in Yellowknife. There were reporters from as far away as London, England; West Germany, and France. The Canadian news corps consisted of reporters from many parts of the country and the Canadian Broadcasting Corporation (CBC) had flown in 10 of its employees for the hearing.

Coroner England, a hardware merchant and local Justice of the Peace, had presided over approximately 100 inquests in a dozen years. This one would be much different. He was already being badgered by the press. His telephone rang non-stop as reporters, attempting to get the jump on their competition, sought out interviews. It would be hectic but no different for him than for the large contingent of legal minds being flown in to handle the case.

Fifty-year-old William Trainor of Ottawa, a former police magistrate for the Yukon Territory, was representing the Federal Justice Department. Red Cavanagh was there on behalf of his client Marten Hartwell. Another Edmonton lawyer, 40-year-old Philip Ketchum, was representing the estate of nurse Judy Hill. He had attended college in Cambridge, England and a friend of his at that time, Chris Brooks, who was reading Medicine, was about to become engaged to be married to the young nurse at the time of her death. Ketchum was a personal friend of Judy Hill, and his family, "really loved her."

There were others.

Toronto lawyer James Karswick, 38, retained by the Inuit Tapirisat (Eskimo Brotherhood), was there to ensure representation for the Inuit victims.

Howard Irving of Edmonton identified his client as Gateway Aviation.

J.R. Slaven of Yellowknife was representing the Territorial Government and Major Armand Desroches, the Department of National Defence. They would be joined later by Gerald Flaherty, an assistant general counsel with the CBC.

Forty-one persons had been subpoenaed to give testimony, and although great interest was already being expressed at what had taken place following the crash, Coroner England repeatedly emphasized that the main business at hand was to determine what had happened leading up to and including the cause of the deaths, not what might have happened to any of the people concerned after death.

Notwithstanding that statement, the throngs that were now beginning to congregate in the lobby of the snowbound city's largest hotel were extremely conscious of the enormous public attention already given the case. The feeling was backed up by the young woman behind the hotel desk who remembered almost too vividly what she had heard when the rescuers returned to that same building after the discovery had been made. It was unspeakable. She returned to her work.

To allow room for the overflow crowd of news media and interested members of the public, arrangements had been made to hold the inquest in the banquet room of the Yellowknife Inn. As the lawyers, witnesses and reporters gathered in the hotel's crowded coffee shop, known as the 'Miners' Mess,' there was already talk of some of the stories that had broken into print while they slept.

The Manager of Gateway's Yellowknife operation, Neal Murphy, had been quoted as denying charges that planes flying in the North do not carry enough rations.

He said that the planes are normally equipped with two survivor kits, "each containing enough food to last two persons 16 days".

It was no secret, however, to those hearing the report that one of the containers was never found.

There was widespread belief that key witness Marten Hartwell would refuse to appear at the inquest. He did not have to as he was outside the jurisdiction of the Coroner's Ordinance Act of the Northwest Territories. In essence, as long as he remained outside the Territories, and at this time he was at his home in Edmonton, Alberta, there was no provision in law that would allow the police to force him to return. Hartwell could not be arrested and extradited from the neighboring province. Thus the talk that he would fail to answer his subpoena, running counter to the knowledge that a room was being held in his name at the hotel, increased as it was learned what his lawyer had said to the press.

"In his statement to police, Hartwell makes reference to consideration of cannibalism," Red Cavanagh was quoted as saying. "I will go that far."

His remarks, published in a Toronto newspaper, fed more

fuel to the speculation that his client would not testify. Cavanagh was quoted as saying that he was afraid that if Hartwell did testify, "the press will crucify him."

The lobby of the hotel quickly filled as the time neared for the inquest to get underway. One hundred ten persons crammed seats reserved for the public. Another 40 stood at the back of the improvised courtroom. As an RCMP Staff Sergeant closed the doors, a sizeable group waited outside in the hope that someone would leave and they would be able to take their place.

The six man jury, all from Yellowknife, slowly filed into the room. Robert O'Connor, Brock Parsons, William Hines, Tony Mrdeza, and Robert Engle were led by jury foreman Duncan Matheson. Five of the all-male panel were known for their extensive flying experience in the North. The sixth member, the only one without a background in aviation, was described as the owner of a local cleaning and janitorial service.

Originally, all the jury members were people experienced in the field of aviation. When one of them turned out to be unavailable at the last moment — just prior to their official swearing-in and identification of the bodies stored in a hangar — the coroner was faced with the prospect of finding a last minute replacement.

Mrdeza, working late in the courthouse, was roped in for duty when he was spotted by Coroner England in the deserted halls of the building.

Star witness and lone survivor Marten Hartwell was conspicuous by his absence. He had been subpoenaed to appear well in advance and even though he wasn't scheduled to testify until the third day of the proceedings, his failure to show-up ahead of time did not sit well with many of the local residents. They wanted to know all that had happened and they wanted to hear it from the one person who could tell them.

Professor David Haley, the Mathematics professor from Acadia University in Nova Scotia, expressed concern as he spoke from his home.

"I intend to protest against the fact that the inquest is an open one which the public can attend," stated the professor. "Poor Marten has been through enough already. I see no reason why he should have to go through this in public. I cannot see why he should be subject to this."

Coroner England, well aware of the history of the Coroner's inquest, perhaps the oldest court in British law which came about in the 11th and 12th centuries to settle the public mind about how a person lying dead had been killed, disagreed.

"There was no way this inquest cannot be public," he said. "The inquest is on behalf of the public. The inquest will be an open one regardless of pressures."

The controversy was already underway.

Coroner England, in his opening remarks, explained that only Crown counsel William Trainor would examine witnesses. Quoting from the Coroner's Ordinance of the Northwest Territories he read in part, "counsel representing Her Majesty may attend at any inquest and may examine or cross examine the witnesses." Explaining that this was "standard practice" the Coroner said that the other lawyers could consult with Mr. Trainor on questions they may wish to ask, "but only Mr. Trainor will examine the witnesses." This meant that the other counsels could only submit suggestions for questions to the Federal Justice Department man. They then had to leave the decision to him as to whether or not he felt it was "worthwhile" to put them in turn, to the witnesses.

Toronto lawyer James Karswick, representing the Inuit victims, was quick to protest. He pointed out the possible disadvantages of the system, "which in this particular inquest are somewhat unfair." There were many widely disparate fields of interest involved in these current proceedings. He maintained that Trainor might not feel questions pertaining to all of them were, "relevant or necessary to cover at all, let alone at length."

Citing the number of government agencies involved in the investigation (The Ministry of Health with regard to evacuation procedures, The Ministry of Transport with respect to aircraft regulations and the Department of National Defence in connection with search procedures) Karswick argued bitterly.

"Here we have a counsel representing these government agencies, not only being the only person, the only counsel that is actively and directly participating in the proceedings, but also having the effectual control to the extent of the questioning and the extent of the investigation. I submit that this represents a real difficulty and one that in my professional submission is not in the best interest of the overall public interest."

The bid was rejected by the Coroner who had the discretion to change the system. He did provide a commitment though that the proposal would be reconsidered if the method of questioning proved unsatisfactory.

There was also a promise from Crown counsel Trainor who said, "I don't intend in any way to cover up, or I hope I am not going to be biased in any way in connection with what my friend referred to as some government agencies. I will do my best to ask the questions which he feels are relevant."

The matter had barely finished when lawyer Philip Ketchum, a tall, lanky individual emanating an air of authority, rose to his feet.

He advised that representations could be expected from him later on to possibly close the court, "out of respect for the family."

Coroner England, who said the matter would be considered when it was raised, was then hit with a formal complaint over the jury's selection.

Lawyer Karswick, emphasizing that native people make up 70 or 80 per cent of the population of the Northwest Territories, charged that no native persons had been included on the jury.

Coroner England, in an explanation based on a section contained in the Coroner's Ordinance Act stated, "in a mining accident we attempt to get mining personnel to sit on the jury. In a construction accident we have to get construction people in this area and in this particular case we have attempted to get people knowledgeable in the aviation industry ..."

Karswick argued, but to no avail.

The first witness had yet to take the stand. The jury would carry out its primary function of determining the cause of death but it wasn't nearly as evident as to how it would do it, whether or not the many other points would be cleared up. It was hoped they would be, but it was now something cast in doubt.

A question of bias and the threat of suppressed evidence had been placed on the record. They were serious misgivings but only time would prove or disprove their accuracy.

Dr. Ernest Edward McCoy, a pediatrician who worked out of the University of Alberta School of Medicine in Edmonton, was called as the first witness. The School of Medicine provides consultants to the Northwest Territories who visit the remote settlements once or twice a year to provide specialized services. Dr. McCoy had been carrying out this consultant work in the community of Spence Bay during November 7th when David Kootook, complaining of abdominal pains, presented himself to the nursing station. It was a miserably cold day with 40 mile per hour winds and visibility reduced by blowing snow when Dr. McCoy, along with the two Spence Bay nurses, Maeve Walsh and Judy Hill, listened to the young lad as he told of the sharp ache.

"We conducted certain examinations on him," testified Dr. McCoy, "and discovered at that point he had a presumptive diagnosis of acute appendicitis. He had had abdominal pain and vomiting since nine that morning."

Dr. McCoy then related how the youngster was sent home for the night, but a mere four hours later, a woman, Neemee Nulliayok, was at the nursing station complaining of gnawing pain. She was 32 weeks pregnant. Since she had a history of spontaneous abortions in the middle of pregnancy, said Dr. McCoy, she had a shirodkar suture inserted during a 72-hour stay in Yellowknife hospital, five months previous. The suture, a flat piece of ribbon, made of mescaline (a synthetic plastic), was inserted deep through the cervix lining, front to back and tied with a knot.

"This suture," said Dr. McCoy, "is the recommended treatment to prevent this (spontaneous abortions) from recurring. It is very effective in treatment of long pregnancies in allowing them to be carried to termination."

"Once the labor pains had begun," he explained, "one either has to do a caesarian section or the suture has to be cut."

The caesarian section, a full-scale operation, was ruled out because the nursing station did not have the necessary surgical system. The only hope was to locate and cut the suture. Afterwards, the infant could be placed in an incubator, but even then if complications had developed the facilities were unavailable.

"The two nurses," said Dr. McCoy, "examined the woman." He did not.

"Miss Walsh and Miss Hill are both trained midwives and I was doing something else in the nursing station when this examination took place," testified the doctor. "I think the question could be raised, should I not have seen that myself?"

He later told the jury that it had been about 20 years since he had participated in a gynecologic practice.

"I don't believe I tried to make myself out as a consultant gynecologist. This is not my function," said the doctor. "I tried to carry out a level of competence but I do not in any way pretend that I am an expert in that sense."

"But in fact you have given some evidence that you felt the two girls were more expert than you?" asked Crown counsel William Trainor.

"Yes sir. I believe that is correct," replied Dr. McCoy.

The responsibility for locating the suture had been placed with the two nurses. It could not be located and the decision was made to evacuate the woman.

"The action," said Dr. McCoy, "coincided with information placed on her chart following the June operation. The instructions were, that if the patient did have premature birth, that she was to be evacuated to Yellowknife."

He related how the suffering continued throughout the

night and into the next morning for both David Kootook and Neemee Nulliayok. The removal of the woman was considered urgent. The case of David was not as bad as that of his aunt and his removal could have waited for one day and perhaps even two days, said the doctor. "Even though I know that 50 per cent of cases of acute appendicitis will resolve themselves spontaneously."

"One cannot know which 50 per cent will respond without operation and which will not. If they did recur again we would probably have a rupture of the appendix and probable death of the patient if he were not treated."

Dr. William Delanor Flatt, the second witness called to testify, was sworn-in. Dr. Flatt, a gynecologist who completed his training at the Toronto General Hospital in 1947, explained that on June 30th he performed an operation on the woman at which time he placed the suture around her cervix. He said this was only done after the procedure had been explained to the patient through an interpreter because she could not understand, as it was outlined in English.

Dr. Flatt, stating that he had done quite a number of the operations, described it as standard procedure, "the best operation."

He told the inquest that this was Mrs. Nulliayok's fourth pregnancy. That the first child lived, and in the cases of the next two pregnancies, the children were born prematurely and did not survive.

Evidence had been given earlier by Dr. McCoy that the woman was 32 weeks pregnant when it was deemed an emergency to rush her to the hospital in Yellowknife.

Now, Dr. William Flatt was asked if there was anything done to ensure follow-up treatment after the June operation.

"I was out of town on July 1st and Dr. O'Donoghue discharged the patient. It was recommended at that time that the patient come to Yellowknife two weeks prior to the expected date of confinement, which would be about January 3rd or approximately then, or if labor did commence at an earlier date, the patient should come to Yellowknife immediately."

A hush fell over the inquest room. Testimony had already been given by Dr. McCoy that the woman was 32 weeks pregnant on November 7th, and now there was testimony that her chart advised the expected date of confinement would be about January 3rd.

If the nursing station waited until the suggested date to advise the woman that she should go into Yellowknife hospital it would have meant that Mrs. Nulliayok would have been approximately 10 months pregnant. It was said to be, highly unusual for medical personnel to be placed in a situation where proper follow-up contact may not occur. At any rate, there was evidence of a gross error and grave danger to a patient dependent upon them for advice because she could not receive adequate care in Spence Bay and had to be moved in lots of time so she would have proper treatment.

Dr. Flatt stepped down from the stand and the next witness to be called was Elizabeth Ann Budd. Miss Budd, a registered nurse in charge of the Cambridge Bay nursing station in the absence of the resident doctor, spoke in a low, nearly inaudible voice. She had been a co-worker of Judy Hill and was now being forced to remember details that were extremely sorrowful. She told the inquest that she had been at the distant settlement of Cambridge Bay for nearly two years. The young nurse then explained how Judy Hill had advised her that the sick patients were being flown in and that she went out to the airport to meet them. She then told of a conversation with Marten Hartwell whose plane had landed at the airport earlier.

"I told him about the situation and that the patients had to be brought to Yellowknife as soon as possible. He said that he had been to Perry River but couldn't get there because of bad weather and had come into Cambridge Bay to refuel. He didn't seem very anxious to go back to Yellowknife. This is what he said to me, that he wasn't too anxious to go back to Yellowknife."

The nurse told the inquest that two pilots, Hartwell with the Beechcraft and Ed Logozar flying a Twin Otter and also employed by Gateway Aviation, decided between themselves that the Hartwell craft would continue on to Yellowknife.

She also confirmed that a DC-3 aircraft, a scheduled flight of NWT Air, was expected in later that afternoon, but it was decided against using the plane because it was often late and did not fly direct to Yellowknife. The larger commercial aircraft could have been used in place of the Beechcraft to move the patients.

"It's usually expected around 6:30 but it is liable to come any time after that," said the nurse.

"Well, you would be surprised if I told you I was going to lead evidence that they arrived at 4:25 that afternoon?" asked Crown counsel Trainor.

"Yes," answered the nurse.

If they had waited less than an hour, the commercial carrier DC-3 would have been in Cambridge Bay.

In concluding, the State Registered nurse from England told the jurors that before the mercy flight departed, she gave Judy Hill six cheese sandwiches, some home-made cookies and a flask of coffee.

The next witness to be sworn-in was Dr. Ali Oktay Uygur who was the Medical Director in charge of the MacKenzie zone. He explained that the area for which he was responsible covered a wide territory, including Spence Bay and Cambridge Bay, and involved a total of 12 nursing stations, five health centres and three medical clinics. He testified that decisions to evacuate patients were usually made only after the nurses consulted with a doctor. Dr. Uygur, who admitted that nurses could decide to evacuate on their own if a doctor was unavailable, explained that there were no written standard procedures to be followed by those in outposts at the time of such crisis. What it boiled down to was that nurses, unable to locate senior personnel for permission to evacuate, could make the decision using their own judgement. Naturally, it would be based on their experience with Arctic conditions.

Dr. Harry Brian Brett was the next to be called to testify. Dr. Brett, the Director of Northern Health Services which covers the entire Northwest Territories and the Yukon Territory, confirmed that there was no written policy to be followed in deciding medical evacuations.

The Edmonton based doctor stated, "one of the reasons it did not come about was the fact that it was the opinion of some of us, if you got out a series of written instructions trying to cover any possibility it could easily lead to paralysis of action."

Although there were no such written procedures at the time of the mercy flight, the death of three and possibly four persons had prompted the government agency into rapid action.

"Now, have you done some re-thinking with respect to medical evacuations and instructions to the nurses?" asked Crown counsel Trainor.

"Yes, there is already in existence a book of instructions regarding emergency evacuation procedures," said Dr. Brett. "I should stress," testified the doctor, "that this is still in draft form and is largely the creation of people who are knowledgeable, not only in medicine but in aviation. In fact, it was just received about one week ago."

The draft document was entered as exhibit number one.

There were more witnesses to be called during the first day.

A member of an oil drilling crew, James LaFleur of Yellowknife, stated that he, along with David Thomas and Marten Hartwell, attempted to fly to Perry River on the morning of November 7th but turned back because of bad weather.

He testified that the same thing happened the next day or only hours before the crucial medical evacuation would take place.

"It was cloudy and you couldn't see very far. You couldn't see anything. He couldn't find the river I guess."

LaFleur also testified that the passenger window of the Beech 18 was continually fogging up.

Mining Engineer, David Thomas of Calgary, then got on the stand to back up this record of the day's events.

"Well, the weather was, I think, around Perry River not too

bad. I think we overshot the target because we couldn't see the ground and we couldn't spend much time looking for Perry River because we were low on fuel."

He explained that as soon as the plane landed back at Cambridge Bay, he was asked by nurse Budd to release the aircraft for the medical evacuation and he agreed to do so. He also had to give permission to Marten Hartwell in the form of releasing the charter.

"He said it's up to me to decide whether they could have the plane or not, and he said he would go as long as I would release him. However, I think he was a little reluctant."

Thomas testified that the day before, there was trouble navigating the plane. "I think he was having trouble picking up Contwoyto Lake beacon. He seemed to point to his earphones and just stick with it and he left me the impression he was having trouble getting his direction from the beacon. This was when he turned around and came back."

The first day of the inquest ended, but not before David Thomas elaborated on his statement that Hartwell appeared hesitant to take the mercy flight. "I think it was because of the weather that he may have been somewhat reluctant to make the flight to Yellowknife."

The barrage of lawyers, charges that the interests of native people were being neglected, and a bid to have reporters and the public barred from hearing certain evidence were all highlights as the story surrounding the tragedy slowly began unfolding. As the overflow crowd shuffled out of the improvised, stuffy inquest room, they were thankful that it was the job of the six-man jury and not theirs to unravel the mystery of the barrens.

The on-again, off-again appearance of Marten Hartwell again came to the forefront in the many stories and rumors circulating in the community. However, as the crowd streamed in for the second day of the hearing, this would soon change. Before the day's first witness had been called, the ability of the inquest to clear up the unknowns surrounding the wilderness crash was again cast into doubt.

In a dramatic courtroom confrontation, minutes before the morning testimony was due to begin, Toronto lawyer Karswick again accused Coroner England and Crown counsel Trainor with frustrating attempts to reveal the entire truth of the circumstances that preceded and followed the crash.

He said the system, whereby only the Crown counsel could ask questions of witnesses, was not working.

"I am stopped from having certain areas which I feel should be explored in greater detail," complained the lawyer, "and I also find that when certain questions or when certain areas are raised or asked to be raised, that they are not done in the manner I would have them. I am not criticizing Mr. Trainor for this but his viewpoint is different from my viewpoint. He is representing the government here, and I am representing the Inuit, and if I could cross-examine I would do it in a different manner."

"Yes, well Mr. Karswick, my ruling in having Mr. Trainor ask the questions of the witnesses and handle this aspect of the hearing was for the purpose of not having the inquiry, the inquest, take on the form or appear to be a trial," said Coroner England.

"There is no one on trial at this inquest and I don't want a lot of objections, a lot of people standing up and objecting to this course or that course or belabored questioning of the witnesses."

"It is just not satisfactory and not acceptable," remonstrated Karswick. "We find that we just can't get at what we feel would be a complete and detailed and proper examination which would have the effect of clearing the air, of clearing a lot of public suspicion and gossip which has been flying around, and under the circumstances I have no alternative but to simply withdraw from these proceedings, and make it clear that as far as the Inuit are concerned, we are not happy with the way this matter is being conducted."

Crown counsel Trainor, taken aback by the strong verbal assault, jumped to his feet to demand that Karswick explain his suggestion of rumor and gossip.

"I don't know what they are, and if there is some basis for those, and he thinks there is," said the Crown counsel, "they should be brought forward."

"My friend is asking me not to submit any law but to give a statement of rumor and gossip," countered Karswick who later expanded on his position. "I am not here because of rumor, I am here because of a right to represent these (the Inuit) families."

A wave of amazement swept through the courtroom as the lawyer publicly withdrew from any further participation. Karswick, as reporters rushed out to file their stories, removed himself from the counsel table. He moved back behind the Bar into the public gallery and within minutes walked out of the courtroom. He then returned to central Canada. The man who had earlier questioned the lack of native representation on the jury had attracted a tremendous public following in the short time he had been in Yellowknife and now he was gone. Nevertheless, it was as though nothing had happened. The hearing simply continued with the only change being an air of relief noticeable from the officials who remained, and of course, there was the lawyer's chair that was now empty. It was as if no one in authority cared and it wasn't until much, much later that day that the questions raised by Karswick were brought back into the spotlight — this time by members of the jury.

"The jury is concerned," stated foreman Duncan Matheson, "now that Mr. Karswick has withdrawn, whether or not the interests of the Eskimo (Inuit) people are being served?"

It was almost as though the question was asked only because it was expected that there would be at least a slight bit of interest shown.

Coroner England replied, "my own opinion is that the interests of the Eskimo (Inuit) people and all people are being served by the inquest generally ..."

The matter ended as quickly as it had been raised and a feeling of disgust seemed to engulf the emotion-filled room. It had been seen as such an apparent, half-hearted attempt that the local people seemed embarrassed because it had been witnessed by those from the outside.

Edward Gordon Logozar took the stand. It was this individual who had been at least partially responsible for convincing Hartwell to take the mercy flight. He himself had an IFRA rating, having reached a level of proficiency and passing official examinations that were necessary before piloting a plane on instruments alone.

He recalled parts of their discussion held on the near deserted landing field.

"I asked Marten if he had come out to pick up this medical evacuation and he said no, he was on another charter," testified Logozar. "I asked him if he would do this trip because we were going to Coppermine and he was a little hesitant at first."

"Was it your opinion," asked Crown counsel Trainor, "that the weather conditions were VFR (Visual Flight Rules) all the way to Yellowknife?"

"They appeared to be VFR, yes," replied Logozar.

Later testimony from a Gateway Aviation official would confirm that Logozar was a senior pilot with the firm and had the authority to ask that the Beech 18 give up its charter and proceed on the rescue mission.

"Did you have any occasion to discuss with Mr. Hartwell," asked Crown counsel Trainor, "the fact that if he took off for Yellowknife at that time that he would be flying in darkness?"

"No, we didn't," replied the pilot.

The testimony brought out one hitherto overlooked factor. With night falling fast it would definitely be pitch dark before the aircraft would reach Yellowknife, but Hartwell obviously aware of this, did not stress to Logozar he was a 'VFR' pilot only and that he must have the ground in sight at all times. Hartwell was reluctant to go. He wanted an excuse and this would have provided the perfect opportunity. It was a valid argument that could not be disputed — why then his silence?

Before concluding his testimony, Logozar passed criticism on the Contwoyto beacon, "I think it should be beefed up. I have always complained about it."

A radio operator on duty at Cambridge Bay on the night of November 8th, Edward Burton Palmer was the next witness. He recounted that there had been difficulties communicating by radio with the pilot, "only a couple of minutes after he had taken off."

Palmer, who was asked about the light conditions at the time of takeoff, replied, "it was getting on towards dusk. When we looked out the window at the station we could see the aircraft but it was getting fairly dark."

Next on the witness stand was Brian McBurney, the other radio operator on shift that evening at Cambridge Bay.

He testified that when Hartwell had been approaching Cambridge Bay, about three minutes before the Beechcraft was due to land, there had been trouble communicating with him. The pilot, he said, then came into the office. He was given an area forecast. At the time he was mainly concerned about icing conditions, having encountered some on the flight down from Yellowknife to Perry River. He was told that there was light to moderate icing forecast for the Cambridge Bay and Yellowknife regions.

The immediate Cambridge Bay conditions also given to Hartwell included the following details. McBurney said, "the weather was estimating the ceiling at 7,000 feet, visibility was 1,500 plus, the weather was calm."

"Did you give him any other weather?" asked Crown counsel Trainor.

"I can't be sure," replied McBurney who added that the weather information for Yellowknife was available on the operator's console and would have been given to the pilot, if he could not see it by himself.

As of 10:30 a.m. the forecast called for cloud based at 1,500 to 2,000 feet above main sea level and topped at 5,000 feet and visibility to be generally one to four miles with light snow. There was also an addendum on the Contwoyto Lake area that visibility could be as low as one-half to one mile with snow.

"His weather would have been the 3 o'clock weather?" asked Crown counsel Trainor.

"That's right," answered McBurney.

The weatherman in Yellowknife, Ronald George Catling who typed up the report, was to contradict the statement.

He testified, "the forecast available to him in Cambridge Bay at the time that he was at the weather office would have been the one issued at 17:30 Greenwich mean time, which is 10:30 in the morning, and the valid period of it is from 11 in the morning until zero-six-zero Greenwich mean time, or 11 o'clock at that time."

The meteorologist related that the forecast which was still in force when Hartwell was filing his flight plan was, "for cloud based at 1,500 to 2,000 feet above mean sea level, and topped at 5,000 feet, and visibility to be generally one to four miles with light snow, with an addendum on the Contwoyto Lake area that visibility could be as low as one-half to one mile with snow. That was the forecast issued at 11 o'clock in the morning and was available at Yellowknife, at Cambridge Bay and other places in the area."

Referring to the forecast calling for cloud based at 1,500 to 2,000 feet above sea level, the meteorologist testified, "a good part of the terrain over that route is as high as 1,500 feet."

As it turned out the forecast issued at 3 p.m., but not in the Cambridge Bay office, was identical. It also proved correct, as weatherman Catling testified that at 7 o'clock on the night of November 8th, Contwoyto Lake reported a ceiling of 1,500 feet. It was an intriguing point.

In his statement to the police, later to be revealed, Hartwell said that the weather office, "had not received the Yellowknife weather, but when I tried to use this as an excuse not to take the flight, Logozar said he had got the weather from another radio station." Logozar's recollection of that part of the conversation differs.

"I asked him if he would do this trip because we were going to Coppermine," said Logozar, "and he was a bit hesitant at first and finally when I went and checked the weather for my own route I came back out and asked him if he had made up his mind whether he would take it or not, or if he wanted me to take it, and he said at this time that he would take it."

"What were the weather conditions that you got when you went in?", asked William Trainor.

Logozar answered, "If I remember right it was 1,500 scattered, 3,000 broken, and two miles with blowing snow."

"And you also at that time got the weather at Coppermine?"

"That's right."

"What was that?"

"Clear," said Logozar.

After Hartwell took off, McBurney made contact twice. The first time he provided a time check which showed the cabin clock in the Beech 18 was five minutes slow. Then, barely a minute after the plane was airborne, radio operator McBurney called the Beechcraft to see if the pilot wanted an ambulance on stand-by for his arrival at Yellowknife.

"Did you get a reply?" asked William Trainor.

"As such," replied the young operator.

"What does that mean?"

"It was hard to hear. I asked him if he did request an ambulance on arrival and he was very hard to read so I had to hold my headphones close to my ears so as to eliminate any background noise. I asked him to confirm if he did want one or not. He confirmed that he did and that was the last contact."

The presence of the next witness had been deemed so important by Coroner England that he postponed the inquest for seven days to ensure that she would be back in the country after vacationing in Australia. Maeve Walsh was the other nurse on duty with Judy Hill during the admission and examination of the two patients, David Kootook and Neemee Nulliayok, at the Spence Bay nursing station prior to evacuation. She reiterated events leading up to the flight already described by Dr. Ernest McCoy.

She also provided vital descriptive evidence concerning the teenager. David she said, reading a document that was prepared in June, was five foot three and one-quarter inches in height and at that time weighed 110 $^3/_4$ pounds. The form was entered as an exhibit.

Sylvester Clyde Bigney, an airplane refueller at Cambridge Bay, testified that he was called out to gas-up CF-RLD on the day of its final run. Explaining that he was not allowed to go on wings or climb on the planes because of compensation regulations, Bigney said he passed the gas hose up to pilot Hartwell who then fuelled the craft.

Ross Douglas Medley, an electronics technician employed on the DEW line, testified that he had been working as a radar operator in Cambridge Bay. He explained that it was normal procedure that airplanes taking off from that locale would be tracked by radar, and in the case of the Beech 18 he was able to view it on the radar scope for 40 to 45 minutes.

"I had him on the radar from about 70 to 75 miles," said Medley. "I just assumed where I lost him on the radar that he would be approximately 2,000 to 3,000 feet ... if he was flying at a higher altitude we would track him out farther. If he had been down lower we couldn't have tracked him out that far."

The mercy flight faded from sight, according to the radar operator, at either 4:30 p.m. or 4:35 p.m.

Long-time experienced northern pilots told the inquest that if the beacon-type radio transmitter aboard the downed Beechcraft had been activated then the craft should have been located within hours of crashing.

Hartwell, in a diary that he made during the horrific 32 days, said the emergency locater transmitter aboard the plane was not found until the day after the crash. He said David discovered it in the snow but it had not gone off on impact and was not working. He wrote that he got the Dart II going on November 11th and left it on for five hours.

Inspector Robert Lauren Fletcher, nicknamed 'the flying Mountie', related in detail his flight of November 8th whereby he conducted the first electronic search for the missing plane. He said the visibility was good and claimed he had never had any problem, in many years of experience, in communicating with the Contwoyto beacon. It was pointed out that his plane was equipped with expensive equipment necessary for police work.

By now, it was Tuesday evening and the atmosphere was ringed with tension. During the two days of proceedings, Crown counsel Trainor had carefully steered the testimony away from any details connected with the morbid details of the case, now so predominant in the minds of so many. The coffee shop and the corridors in the Yellowknife Inn buzzed with talk. As Wednesday morning dawned, lawyers continued to plot their course in the confines of their hotel rooms while hordes of news reporters awaited developments. For some reason, everyone felt that this would be the day. Northerners, bundled in warm clothing for protection against the bitter elements, were quickly filling the hotel lobby outside the inquest room. Many had been hanging onto every word during the original two days of testimony and they now refused to miss what they fully expected was only a short time away. They rapidly passed through the small corridor leading to the banquet room and were quick to descend upon choice seats once the doors were swung open.

Captain Keith Gathercole, the searchmaster, now took the stand. He confirmed that Marten Hartwell had only a Visual Flight Rating. He had taken the mercy flight in conditions that were not good for VFR flying, where a pilot had to see the ground at all times. Weather conditions on the day the Beech 18 left Cambridge Bay on the ill-fated journey made this difficult if not impossible, Captain Gathercole testified.

This was due to the fact that there was a low cloud ceiling, ice crystals in the air and light snow.

Once again, pilot Hartwell's wisdom in undertaking the flight at all came under a doubtful light. Why had he gone ahead regardless? There was an atmosphere of frustration in the courtroom as reporters, jury members and the public came to the realization that this question might never be answered under oath.

Hartwell, the main witness, was still not there.

The first photographs of the crash site were shown to the packed inquest. Seventeen color slides of the area, taken by RCMP Constable Ron Kingdon, were projected onto a screen behind the Coroner's desk. They showed the trail of the plane's destructive descent and how it had sheared off the tops of many tall, snow-capped fir trees. It looked almost as though a number of lumberjacks had trimmed the upper portion of the trees to provide sunlight in the clearing where the crumpled Beechcraft now rested. One slide showed the lone survivor standing in the isolated clearing as rescue craft hovered overhead, another the makeshift tent where his lonely existence took place, and others the battered fuselage and smashed cockpit of the aircraft. An attempt was made by Constable Kingdon to read the setting on the pilot's radio but two of the digits on the battered instrument panel were indecipherable. Fourteen 8x10 black and white photographs, which were not shown to the press or public, were then passed around among the jury panel and counsel. Identified by Constable Kingdon, the primary investigating officer from Yellowknife, these again showed the site of the crash strewn with branches from the deformed fir trees that had been mowed down by the plane in its last erratic moments before slamming into the ground. Four close-up pictures showed the position and state of the bodies at the crash site and at the time they were received at the pathology laboratory.

Following these exhibits, Crown counsel Trainor rose to call Marten Hartwell to the stand.

The room suddenly went deathly silent.

This was the day the pilot had been ordered to appear by subpoena.

There was no answer.

Then, as the heads of spectators, reporters, and jurymen scanned the back of the room for the bearded survivor, after days of skirting the issue, Red Cavanagh came out with what he had known all along. The statement was dramatic but not totally unexpected. His client, said Cavanagh, would not be appearing.

"The memory of the things that have happened is very painful to him," said Cavanagh, "he feels that speaking about these things will cause distress, not only to himself, but to the relatives of the deceased."

He told the inquest that his client was aware that many journalists were in Yellowknife and felt his appearance would result in "added publicity without added knowledge" since these things had already been said to the police.

"I do not rule out if it becomes evident that there was something that needed explanation that only he could give that he might come, but I think that the authorities have all the evidence and everything that Mr. Hartwell knows, and under the circumstances I think that the police can use some of his statements to put his evidence here for this inquiry."

Cavanagh added a passionate plea based on his client's state of health.

"He is presently in a cast on his right leg from his foot to his crotch. He can get about, but with difficulty, on crutches, but mostly he is using a wheelchair and it would be difficult for him to travel, which is another consideration."

The jury members took strong exception. As the only living eyewitness they claimed that it was imperative for Hartwell to be placed on the stand where he could be questioned freely. The vehemence of their opinion did not alter the situation. The survivor was outside the jurisdiction of the Northwest Territories and could not be compelled to appear. If necessary, Cavanagh suggested, his client could answer any questions prepared by the jury, by telephone. For the jury, charged with deliberating on all issues surrounding the crash, the proposed procedure was a strange, ineffectual method of obtaining vital evidence. But they were powerless to do more.

RCMP Inspector Tom Venner, responsible for acquiring an official 'warned statement' from the pilot, was then sworn-in. He began to recount how he had gone about the task two weeks before. But almost as quickly as he had begun to explain, he abruptly stopped. At this crucial moment, with all eyes focussed on the witness stand, it was noiseless.

The tape on the recording machine used by court reporter Everett Tingley had run out. A rather perplexed look crossed the face of Tingley, a cherubic character who gave the impression of being a likeable, individual who was unused to being placed in such a delicate situation. Afterall, this appeared as though it would be the most profound moment of testimony and it was a somewhat awkward development to say the least. Tingley, described earlier as "an expert reporter", soon had the machine going again and indicated the testimony could continue.

Inspector Venner, who had been waiting patiently to submit the evidence which had taken such a long time to obtain, confirmed that he had gone to a suite located in a walk-up apartment structure in Edmonton. In the company of the pilot, Red Cavanagh, and Susan Haley, he said this is where he had obtained the statement and had read it aloud to ensure there was no misunderstanding.

He then read Marten Hartwell's statement.

"On November the 7th I started out for Swan Lake on Perry River, 510 miles northeast of Yellowknife, with two passengers," the statement began.

It went on to explain that he encountered poor conditions on that day and also the following day when he was asked to take the mercy flight. He explained, "I was not eager to go, in fact I did not want to go, and I had encountered icing conditions again on the way up, and did not want to run into them at night."

There was also mention of problems in receiving signals from the Contwoyto Lake beacon. All seemed to go well until Contwoyto Lake, about an-hour after takeoff, when the beacon faded. Yet, he was still not worried because he believed the beacon was unreliable. He then tried to take in the distant signals from Yellowknife, trying to check his bearings, but the only signals he got soon faded. He then received some directional indications from Fort Franklin and Fort Reliance but they were obscured by static. In a last ditch effort, he descended, and even though he knew he was off course, did not think he was lost.

"I was not worried I might not ultimately find Yellowknife," said Hartwell, "I had enough fuel for six and one-half hours."

As the craft plunged into a band of darkness it appeared that he had been successful. Almost immediately there was a loud, clear signal coming through from the distant Wrigley beacon.

"I looked outside the plane, forward and down and couldn't see any rise in the ground," the statement continued. "The time was 6:12 p.m. mountain standard time. I then got out the map so as to check the Morse code signal for Wrigley, unfolded it, and turned on the reading lamp. A few seconds later the crash must have occurred, since I can't remember anything else."

The details of the crash, with the bodies of those on board being hurtled like matchsticks, were horrible to those who listened in wonder. As testified on previous days, not everyone was strapped down in the plane. It would have taken a mere distraction of 60 seconds for the plunge into the hillside. In the earlier detailed and exhaustive technical evidence, there had been nothing to indicate that the seat belts of either the pilot or the nurse had been fastened as the plane plummeted to earth.

"Seatbelts, as we arrived at the scene, were undone", testified MOT official Alphonse Froehler. "There were no buckle or stretch marks to indicate that these belts were fastened at the impact."

Inspector Venner continued reading from the statement. He told of the cold, hunger and endless waiting. He confirmed that there had been an admittance by Hartwell that he and David Kootook discussed cannibalism but the boy did not want anything to do with it.

"I asked him if he would eat the bodies and he said no. We had talked about eating the bodies some days earlier and he would have done it then, but I did not feel like it. He said then that he would not eat his aunt because she was always good to him."

It was not long after this that Red Cavanagh objected.

He asked that the final two pages of the 24-page handwritten statement not be made public. The request was rejected by Coroner England. It was now nearing the supper-hour and many of the spectators were becoming restless. It appeared as though a long legal battle would ensue and it was again doubtful whether the entire story would be divulged.

The inquest was adjourned until later in the evening. The issue would be appealed to Mr. Justice William Morrow of the Northwest Territories Supreme Court. Shortly afterwards, the lawyers convened in a small courtroom in the modern government building across the road from the Yellowknife Inn. There, before Mr. Justice Morrow, an application was filed for a writ of prohibition in connection with the evidence. There were arguments put forward by the various lawyers. Some wanted explicit descriptions provided by Hartwell placed into evidence at the inquest. Others maintained it would be harmful if the information became public.

There were deletions from the original statement and the lawyers returned to the public hearing. When the inquest reconvened, it was almost as if an Academy Award winning show was premiering. Spectators crammed the banquet room. They stood five and six deep at the back of the long hall. Furtive glances were cast around the room by some who appeared ill at ease by being present. Others, who had brought small children to watch and listen to the proceedings, acted as though there was nothing wrong, as if they were taking the family out for a night's entertainment to see a Walt Disney movie. A middle-aged woman, who had not missed a moment of the hearing since it began, chuckled to some members of the press as she absentmindedly continued her knitting. She thought she had a secret and was sharing it in her own simple way. A drunk was escorted out of the room. He had been stumbling around in the back making a nuisance of himself. It provided comic relief for those who welcomed the diversion from the seriousness of the proceedings.

Inspector Venner once again took the stand. He was reminded by Crown counsel Trainor that he was still under oath and he acknowledged what he knew to be the obvious.

In a calm, quiet voice, the sombre-faced police officer resumed his reading of the pilot's statement.

"After David was dead my will to live was reawakened. I began to consider what I could do. In the afternoon I crawled out of the tent, got my crutches and stumbled down to the next tree where I expected there would be lichens. I took the axe to bring some firewood to the tent. The tree was about 12 yards away and the snow was trampled and packed down, so it was the easiest tree to get to. In spite of that I was completely exhausted with tremendously aching feet and trembling from exhaustion and pain when I got to it. I had to rest sitting down to gather some strength before I could do anything further. After a while, I chopped off the lower branches which were dry and had some lichens on them. Took crutches and branches under one arm and crawled on my knees back to the tent. The whole operation took almost two hours. I recognized that I could not continue to do that. I made a fire and melted snow and made a soup of the lichens on one branch. No more than a mouthful. At least I then had something warm in my stomach after three days. I began to think about what I could do again. I knew that since I could not manage to gather enough lichens to live, I could not possibly ever make it to the lake to get fish.

I needed something, food, to fill the gap from now to the day that my legs could carry me to the lake, and from here on I think it is clear to the authorities what I did and I won't go through the emotional side of the experience once again. I am still trying to forget this and probably will never succeed."

"Did you eat, consume some of the flesh from the body of Judy Hill?", asked Inspector Tom Venner.

"Yes. Nobody else did. David didn't because I started eating flesh after David was dead."

There were only muffled gasps to break the eery silence. Reactions of loathing, sadness and disbelief were evident in the room that felt like it was rapidly closing in. The extraordinary story had been told. The misery during the lonely days and nights in the sub-zero temperatures, and the terror that had taken place, seemed unreal. A sickening, weak feeling enveloped the room like a virus.

In the wake of this major development, pilot Hartwell was soon to make his first public appearance since the inquest began.

Earlier, by way of explanation for his client's frustrating absence, Red Cavanagh had described the pilot's condition. Although admittedly the only living witness to the events that took place in the snows, he was, Cavanagh said, encased in a cast from crotch to right foot and travel would be extremely difficult.

Two hours later, in Edmonton, the bearded survivor overcame these handicaps to reach the 27th floor of Edmonton's ultra-modern AGT (Alberta Government Telephones) building. Here, in lawyer Cavanagh's luxurious suite of offices, he appeared before television cameras for the purposes of his own, hastily convened news conference.

The press gathering had been planned well in advance as had the decision that Hartwell would not be appearing at the inquest. In actuality, it was decided even before the first day of the hearing, despite the formal announcement coming in such a theatrical manner on the third day, that the sole survivor would not be going to Yellowknife. Now, he travelled across the city of Edmonton to deliver one of two statements prepared with the help of professor David Haley. It would later be revealed that one of the statements was longer than the other and in the event the part about eating human flesh had been ruled non-admissible at the inquest, then the bottom portion would have been deleted. The plan, although prepared far in advance, faltered somewhat when Professor Haley and his daughter Susan failed to notify all of the local news agencies. As a result, only a handful of reporters were present when, in precise, mildly accented English, the survivor began to read from the text that was compiled even before the inquest had begun.

"There was no way out but to eat human flesh and this I did. It distresses me and probably others to talk more about this, but I do want to stress that it was only I who did this and that only after David Kootook's death."

He explained that he had given a full statement to the RCMP and had not made any public statements about the events because, "the memory of them is painful to me. I also feel that speaking about these things will cause distress to the relatives of the people who died."

Sitting in a wheelchair, with his right foot in a heavy cast, he continued to read his statement which included a quote from Dr. Knud Rasmussen's book, ACROSS ARCTIC AMERICA.

"Many people have eaten human flesh. But never from any desire for it, only to save their lives, and that after so much suffering that in many cases they were not fully sensible of what they did."

In a flat, serious voice with only occasional tremors disclosing the tension or nerves erupting beneath the surface, he went on, "but we who have endured such things ourselves, we do not judge others who have acted in this way, though we may find it hard, when fed and content ourselves, to understand how they could do such things. But then again, how can one who is in good health and well-fed expect to understand the madness of starvation. We only know that every one of us has the same desire to live."

No one questioned the human desire to survive. Apart from the few hardened critics who indicated that an heroic death by starvation would have been preferable under the circumstances, the feeling most commonly expressed was one of awe that an individual, especially one who was an admitted vegetarian, had been able to force himself to eat human flesh at all. It had been learned, though this was not brought out nor covered in detail at the inquest, that 39 pounds of flesh had been missing from the body of the dead nurse.

An estimated 10 pounds were found by authorities. According to Hartwell's statement to the police, young David Kootook died on the night of December 1st and on the following day the pilot had gone through his agonizing afternoon trek to obtain lichens for that day's meal which put something warm in his stomach for the first time in three days. It was only after this, he said, that his 'reawakened' survival task began. In the course of seven days, he was rescued on December 9th, in spite of a stomach that would have undergone severe shrinkage due to an inadequate diet, his intake, based on the disclosed information, was abundant.

Apart from the assault on the senses, the flesh itself had to be thawed each day in the meagre warmth of the pilot's sleeping bag and consumed uncooked. Most people would be reluctant to eat raw meat under any circumstances. In Hartwell's case, one could only respect and wonder at the determination involved.

Marten Hartwell refused to answer reporters' questions. Sitting upright in his wheelchair, with his girlfriend Susan Haley near his side, he was whisked from the office by professor David Haley to an undisclosed destination.

It was from this location the next morning, while testifying by telephone without the protection of the Canada Evidence Act, that Hartwell added more information to an excruciating ordeal that already was one of seemingly limitless proportions.

He told Inspector Venner that he had complained previously about some of the aircraft's equipment which had never been repaired. He was quoted as saying that when he brought the matter to the attention of his employer he was told the deficiencies would be corrected but they were not.

The testimony was later refuted by Marcel Rainville, a former Gateway Aviation aircraft engineer, who said there had been some verbal complaints but nothing in writing. Rainville, who said he signed the aircraft out, insisted that both he and Hartwell concluded, the day before the final flight, that the Beechcraft was airworthy.

A sudden murmur went through the room when Inspector Venner read out Hartwell's statement concerning his night flying qualifications. The former Luftwaffe pilot said that he had a total of 100 night flying hours to his credit, half of which had taken place in Germany during the vital World War II years, 1944-45.

In response to other questions, Hartwell said that there had been no gun aboard the plane and that he did not know when the emergency equipment, including survival rations, had last been checked. The ration box was full, he said, apart from the regulation package of pilots' biscuits, which he maintained were missing.

In later testimony, Gateway Aviation official Doug Rae would tell the jury that the matter of the gun and the rations being on board was the responsibility of the aircraft engineer and the pilot.

The jury also received an indirect complaint from pilot Hartwell that his Dart II, Emergency Locater Transmitter, did not work properly. He said it appeared to be broken. It was this same device that was eventually responsible for the pilot's rescue, although, the jury was told that when it was picked up by one of the rescuers, the antenna fell off. The certainty that it was working so well at the time of rescue was emphasized.

Hartwell also criticized the radio beacon at Contwoyto Lake that he had depended on for his course during the medical evacuation.

"The Contwoyto beacon should be taken out because nobody should be allowed to think they can rely on it. It might well be replaced with another beacon, but if so it should be equipment superior to the equipment that is there now."

Further ghastly details of Hartwell's 32-day vigil in the snows were to be provided. Letters written by the German pilot and young David Kootook were read out by interpreters and entered as evidence.

The boy's letter to his parents was written during the first week of the nightmare.

It was scripted in syllabics and translated by the authorities. The entire letter, formed within days of the crash and long before the teen's death, was to his mother and father ...

Few days ago we got to Cambridge Bay. We were going to Yellowknife. The airplane fell. When this happened Neemee died and the nurse. The pilot's legs are broken, he cannot walk. I am alright. We fell between Yellowknife and Cambridge Bay, on the hills. In a few more days, on the fourteenth, the pilot wants me to walk to Yellowknife. So I must try and walk. I pray to God that I will see you again. We eat all the time, the pilot and I. There is just two of us. We have white man's food (dried food). The food is in a box, the box is just a bit bigger than my red suitcase. The weather was bad yesterday and today is foggy. Johnny Kovalah and Lena, give them a kiss for me. We cut wood with an axe and we make fire. There is just me and the pilot here. Neemee and the nurse died when the airplane fell. There was four of us. I will see you again in Spence Bay or in Heaven. I try to pray, I do not feel cold in the day time, only at nights. We have * five thick sleeping bags. Two of them we use for a tent and three to sleep in, and another for a mattress. Today we have been here four days. The pilot's legs are broken. I am fine. I can walk. Give Johnny Kovalah and Lena a kiss for me. Yellowknife is far away from here and I am going to try and walk there. The pilot wants me to walk there. I am finishing writing now. I do not have any more writing paper.

It was signed, Davidie Pessurajak Kootook.

Written a few days after the crash, the sole communique from David Kootook to reach the outside world, revealed how quickly the rations were being used. It also told what the senior Hartwell expected of the youngster who was fully prepared to follow orders. He would even go so far as undertaking a hopeless trek to the Territorial capital in whatever direction the pilot thought it might be. The location was 250 miles northwest of Yellowknife.

David Kootook ran out of writing paper. Marten Hartwell did not.

"When you received this letter, I will be dead," he wrote to his son Peer Herrmann in Cologne, West Germany.

"I have had an accident on November 8, '72 and I am still laying in the bush with broken legs. Have no more food. Please

---

*RCMP confirm there were a total of six sleeping bags. David mentioned a total of five but listed six.

forgive me my sins."

The letter, which told his son that he should have $3,000 of his father's savings and the rest should be given to his father's closest companion Susan Haley to "pay his debts", concluded, "I am wishing you all the best and remember me. In my heart I was not all that bad."

Next came a message addressed to Gateway Aviation, Hartwell's employer.

"Legs definitely broken. No more food. See you in Heaven," he wrote in a note dated November 22nd.

The letter, containing a number of entries, was really a diary. He predicted death by starvation for both himself and the youngster if they were not found. The pilot said he believed he was 100 to 120 miles from Yellowknife and off course. He was actually about 180 miles off course and 250 miles northwest of Yellowknife.

The last entry was dated November 30th, nine days before he was rescued. It was also the final day of life for David Kootook.

"Still alive. David is going to die tomorrow and I two or three days later. No food. My legs don't carry me yet and lichen is not around here. Amen. Marten."

The pilot's grim prophecy was to prove chillingly accurate. David Kootook died within hours of the foretelling passage.

Coroner Walter England announced that copies of the letters and translations would be made available to those requiring them, during the afternoon break. He then glanced at Crown counsel William Trainor as if to seek approval.

"As always, I am in favor of full public disclosure," said Mr. Trainor.

The courtroom erupted into laughter.

A Canadian Forces physician, Dr. Warren Edward Harrison, took the stand and explained that he examined the survivor at the Yellowknife hospital following his rescue.

"His clothing was dirty ... his hair was long, unkempt, matted, and dirty," stated Dr. Harrison.

The Armed Forces physician, asked for his diagnosis at that

time, testified, "I believe he had a broken left knee, possibly something with his left ankle, and a broken right ankle."

"Well, what about the ability of a person with fractures of this kind to walk?" asked Crown counsel Trainor.

"He would not be able to walk," answered the doctor.

The autopsy reports on the three victims were then scheduled to be read into evidence by Dr. Laurier Boutin. However, only selected portions were entered verbally and there was no further attempt by the Crown to seek out additional data contained in the fact-filled documents. Reporters were refused copies of the autopsy reports.

James Karswick, lawyer for the Inuit victims, whose repeated requests by letter and telephone to the authorities were thwarted, was unable to obtain copies of the autopsies relating to his clients.

In the portions admitted, Dr. Boutin noted that David Kootook lost about 35 pounds during the 23 days that he survived following the crash.

"The body weighed 75 pounds, in fact 75 ^{1}/$_2$ pounds stated the doctor. "On observation of the body, it was noted that the body was greatly emaciated, the ribs standing out, the abdomen was scaphoid, that means it was concave."

"Concave?" asked Crown counsel Trainor.

"Yes," replied the pathologist, "and the facial features showed that the eyes were deeply sunken into the skull and the malar bone, the cheek bone, was very prominent with depressions ..."

Although he was enroute to the hospital with what had been diagnosed as apparent acute appendicitis; when he died, David had in reality been suffering from a penetrating stomach ulcer, the autopsy report revealed.

The contents of his stomach, testified the doctor, showed that he had been trying to exist on a diet of, "lichens, spruce needles, wild cranberry leaves, carbonized berries, assorted moss leaves, part of a walnut, assorted pieces of bark and wood, and pieces of fibrous material, possibly synthetic ..."

It was later speculated that the boy found the walnut while

scrounging around inside the battered fuselage for cigarette butts. According to Hartwell, the boy liked to smoke.

"Now, are you able, as a result of your examinations of this body to tell us the cause of death?" asked the Crown counsel.

"The cause of death," testified the doctor, "can be inferred from great emaciation demonstrated on this body and certainly starvation would be a very significant factor."

Mrs. Neemee Nulliayok, suffering from premature labor complications, died of a broken neck.

"My conclusions as a result of this examination pertaining to the injury, the spinal fracture, is that this would be the most likely cause of the lady's death," said Dr. Boutin.

"The child she was carrying, a baby girl eight months developed, would have died within minutes of the mother's death," he added.

The pathologist revealed that English nurse Judy Hill died, "almost instantaneously after impact. The cause of death was from injuries directly related to skull fractures," he said.

The majority of the following testimony consisted mainly of detailed and exhaustive technical reports from investigative teams assigned to study the crash by the Ministry of Transport.

When questioned, one MOT official said, "given the same circumstances for flying the Beechcraft under the existing weather conditions on November 8th, I would have been apprehensive."

Another MOT official, Jock Brindle, told the jury it was illegal for Hartwell to carry passengers on a night flight, or on any assignment that would require him to have a plane up after nightfall.

He said it was wrong even in an emergency because the pilot was licensed for visual flight rules only, in which the ground must be kept in sight at all times. He could not fly by instruments alone. The jury was told that common sense had to prevail even in emergency situations.

Afterwards, a Ministry of Transport official who asked that his name not be used, told reporters that pilot Hartwell might be subject to either temporary or permanent removal of his license for violations of air regulations.

There was evidence that the artificial horizon aboard the Beech showed poor workmanship at its last overhaul, testimony that magnetic compasses are notoriously unreliable in the far North because of the closeness to the North Magnetic Pole, and information read into the record that the death plane didn't carry an air almanac. The text, without which astro compasses are ineffectual, could possibly have reduced the seriousness of the navigation problems faced by pilot Hartwell, but then the jury was told that the aircraft did not have such a compass.

Doug Rae, the operations manager for Gateway Aviation, took the stand.

As Hartwell's employer, his testimony was an important part of the proceedings. "Hartwell," said Rae, "was not to fly at night." The testimony came in response to a question raised by Crown counsel Trainor who asked if the company had any standard instructions to pilots.

"The only instructions that I issued to Mr. Hartwell," replied Rae, "were, I did not want him flying this Beech 18 at night."

"Oh," pondered Trainor, "when did you tell him this?"

"Approximately two weeks prior to the accident when I was in Yellowknife," answered Rae.

He later told the jury that the order not to fly at night was given in the same hotel that was now the scene of the inquest.

"Did he seem to understand you?" asked Trainor.

"I had no reason to believe otherwise," testified the man who had hired Hartwell.

Among the last witnesses to testify was Neal Murphy who was the Yellowknife base manager for Gateway Aviation. He said Hartwell was familiar with the lake 12 miles from where he crashed. Murphy claimed the pilot had landed on the lake three months previously and had flown extensively in the area in the months leading up to the fatal mercy flight. The Gateway official also testified that he had given Hartwell specific instructions, the day before the crash, how to react in adverse weather conditions.

Referring to icing, low weather, and poor visibility that Hartwell reported encountering November 7th, Murphy testified, "my instructions were to him to the effect not to attempt another trip until he had at least a 2,500 feet ceiling and 10-mile visibility, and I explained why."

"Did he seem to understand?" asked Trainor.

"Yes he did," replied Murphy.

"Did he agree with your instructions?"

"Obviously not."

And yet another witness, Gordon Dale Raymond, a young employee with Gateway Aviation, told the jury that the ration box containing enough food for two people to last 16 days, was indeed in the aircraft.

He also raised the possibility that there may have been a second such kit on board. If so, the vital life sustaining food so very necessary at the deserted crash site, probably was at that very moment still buried under several feet of snow.

Very few remained in the hotel based courtroom as the inquest came to an abrupt close. The crowds seemed to gradually diminish from the peak they reached a few days earlier when the insanity of the days leading to cannibalism came out publicly. Those who were not there did not hear what was perhaps the most critical evidence to be given. It was contained in a letter that Hartwell had written to his girlfriend and it was now, with the exception of "personal extracts," being read into the record.

It quoted the pilot as saying the sky was clear and he could see for about two miles, but because his Automatic Direction Finder was not working, he reduced altitude in an attempt to get his bearings. He also explained that the only reason he had taken the trip was because the flight was of an urgent nature.

"It is very urgent to get one of them into the hospital, so I fly at night, and while I was low we ran into this hill. It was all my own fault, it shouldn't have happened."

The final portion of the letter read into evidence was dated November 29th, "still alive, but David gave up. He might die tomorrow, and I two or three days later. No food at all. Live for a while on lichen. My legs don't carry me yet ..."

A long wait was anticipated before the jury would emerge from sifting through the reams of lengthy, and for the most part, complex information. It was possible their recommendations would call for criminal proceedings to be launched.

It was some three and one-half hours later that the jury re-entered the long hall, now nearly deserted compared with the overflowing numbers it held during the early days of the hearing.

Jury Foreman Duncan Matheson rose and began reading the verdict.

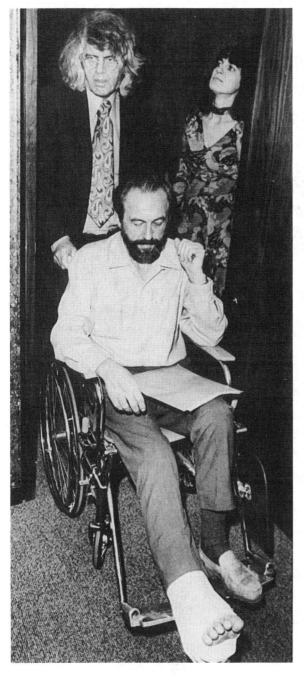

NEWS CON-
FERENCE —
The survivor be-
ing wheeled into
a meeting with
the press. With
him were pro-
fessor David
Haley and his
daughter Susan
— Hartwell's
girlfriend.

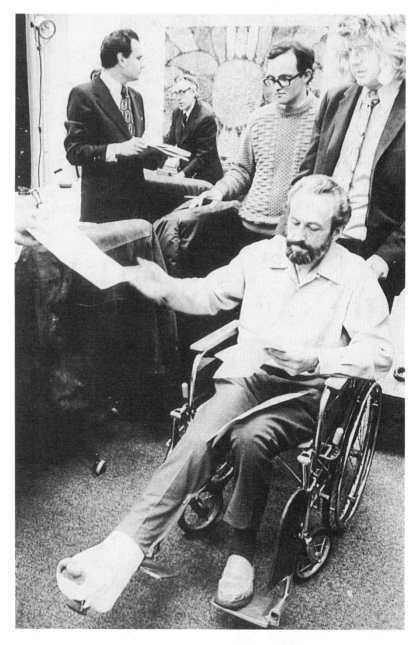

DOCUMENT — Distributed to reporters.

STATEMENT—Read to the assembled representatives of various news agencies.

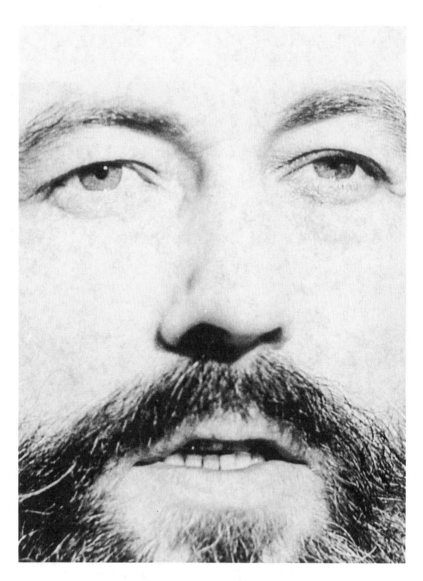

CLOSE-UP — Taken at the 1973
media conference.

Part Two

SURVIVAL

9

1 ... *The jury feels strongly that Marten Hartwell had a moral obligation as the pilot in command of the crashed aircraft to appear at the Coroner's inquest into the death by injury of his passengers, and to come forward as the only surviving witness in the death by starvation of David Kootook.*

2 ... *The jury is unanimous and feels strongly that recognition should be given David Kootook in saving the life of pilot Marten Hartwell and commends his bravery during this ordeal.*

3 ... *The jury is satisfied that inexperience in flying the Beechcraft at night by Marten Hartwell contributed to the crash of CF-RLD.*

4 ... *The jury is satisfied that all of the instruments necessary for the night flight were not in proper working condition and this contributed to the crash of CF-RLD.*

5 ... *We recommend immediate action to initiate the provision of contemporary facilities at Contwoyto Lake to include the following:*

— An NDB (Non-Directional Beacon) with a minimum output of 1,000 watts.

— Establishment of an airstrip large enough to accommodate DC-3 aircraft.

— A VOR-DME (Very High Omni-range and Distance Measuring Equipment) installation to complete the low level and victor airway to Cambridge Bay.

— Full meteorological facilities including upper air soundings.

— The operation of the Contwoyto Lake Station to be placed in the hands of the appropriate MOT (Ministry of Transport) branch or branches rather than the continuance of its operation on a contract basis as is the case at present.

6 ... We further recommend that each nursing station and health centre be equipped with high-frequency single side band radios to ensure communication with one another and with a central station in Yellowknife.

7 ... The jury recommends that the MOT (Ministry of Transport) take immediate action to ensure that Air Almanacs are readily available from a Canadian address to pilots in Canada.

8 ... The jury recommends that Northern Health Services medical facilities at Cambridge Bay be upgraded to that of a hospital as soon as possible.

9 ... The jury unanimously commends and recognizes the high standard of devotion to duty displayed by Judith Hill.

The jury foreman was not finished. There were still an additional nine recommendations from juror Robert O'Connor. They included:

1 ... That regulations requiring the mandatory installation of emergency locater transmitters in all aircraft be expedited.

2 ... That the words, "Check your ELT (Emergency Locater Transmitter) armed", follow final communications between airport towers or air-radio facilities and aircraft departing on all across country flights.

3 ... That a system of close control over electronic emergency locater operation, use and maintenance be adopted, as well as with respect to other emergency equipment.

4 ... That examination of all ELT's (Emergency Locater Transmitters) involved in aircraft accidents be implemented by the appropriate authorities, regardless of their performance in said accident.

5 ... That aeronautical topographical charts be clearly marked as to the date of the base edition, aeronautical information and magnetic variation, as opposed to the system in use at present.

6 ... That consideration be given to expediting the implementation of A.N.O. (Air Navigation Order) series VII No. 3, and a system of standardized personnel files and training records be adopted as part of this A.N.O.

The 36-year-old jury member, the owner of a Yellowknife based Helicopter company, later explained that the navigation order pertained to regulating the day to day operation of small carriers and included provision for crew training.

7 ... That consideration be given by the responsible authorities to closer control over the use and maintenance procedures related to both aircraft radio equipment and instrumentation.
8 ... Ensure that those aircraft intended to be operated in the area of compass unreliability be appropriately equipped.
9 ... And finally, that the attention of all be drawn to Chapter 9 of the Royal Commission on Health Services, 1965.

O'Connor, who had been living in the North since 1959 and started Aero Arctic Limited in 1968, said the final recommendation called for study to be given the suggestion of a comprehensive flying health care service linking various northern communities. He added that what he also had in mind here is that an examination be carried out on the feasibility of establishing a telecommunication system that would provide nursing stations with an independent outside link operable, on a 24-hour basis.

It was over. Six days of exhaustive testimony and now the findings.

Jury foreman Matheson, one of a number of legendary pilots in the Northwest Territories, told reporters, "it was lack of experience. It's a tough country to fly in the winter time at night. That's why the accident happened. He went down when he should have gone up. Navigation instruments were quite important but the trip could still have been done if he'd gone up. The instruments weren't in perfect shape but an experienced man still could have navigated the trip ..."

Crown counsel Trainor, asked if the ruling of pilot inexperience and improperly working instruments constituted negligence as far as the Justice Department was concerned, replied, "the jury said it's negligence. It's a fact finding. I personally don't think there's much doubt that it is negligence. Certainly!"

He added, "negligence can be criminal or civil ... it doesn't mean there is going to be some criminal proceeding flowing from this ..."

He told reporters there is "no present intention" of bringing about any charges relating to the offering of indignities to human remains.

The Crown counsel agreed that there was something wrong with a system that allowed the only living eyewitness the opportunity of not appearing, "that's right, there is a defect," and said he would be bringing it to the attention of the proper authorities.

The loophole resulted in testimony by telephone from Marten Hartwell, an unheard of situation, but rationalized by Mr. Trainor who told the post-inquest news conference, "the jury and the Coroner felt they should get evidence in the best way that was possible and Mr. Hartwell wasn't here, so that was the best way possible."

Lawyer Red Cavanagh's version of the telephone testimony was straightforward. "The long distance calls were paid for by the Territorial Government. We made two phone calls at the request of the Crown. One of them was 45 dollars and the other would be about 31 dollars because the combination was about 76 dollars. It was a helluva lot cheaper than dragging witnesses all over the country."

He was critical of two major points that developed during the lengthy inquiry.

Referring to Justice William Morrow's decision to allow certain portions of Hartwell's statement to be read into evidence, lawyer Cavanagh said, "I think his decision to order those questions be admitted as part of the evidence was wrong in law."

He was also critical of the jury make-up, saying, "I think the Coroner's Ordinance of the Northwest Territories is defective in that it has a stipulation that the jury be composed of six male members. That contravenes the Canadian Bill of Rights, on that ground we might have been able to apply for an injunction and stop the inquest."

Crown counsel Trainor responded, "I do not think there is any doubt about the fact that the Bill of Rights provides that there should not be discrimination on the basis of sex, and the reference to the jury consisting of males is probably a contravention of the Act."

William Trainor had a tremendous responsibility in guiding the inquest, and the manner in which he carried out the task won praise from lawyer Cavanagh.

"He was trying to do two things. Conduct the inquest and show clearly what part the Federal government had to do with it as there had been lots of criticism on the search and rescue. I was impressed with the evidence and I thought they did a helluva job.

They also wanted to dig into the medical evacuation and the doctors showed that was done rather hastily. Also, they wanted to inquire into navigational aids to show what they were and how they worked and so on. Trainor was trying to hold down on the detail of cannibalism. He wanted to establish that it did occur, but he was holding down on the detail."

The view was backed up by one of the rescuers.

"We were briefed what to say and what not to say, which was in effect until Wednesday night when the cannibalism came out. Prior to that we were told only to talk about the search and rescue, period. It was a play."

From his office in Toronto, James Karswick, the Inuit legal representative who walked out of the proceedings in Yellowknife, offered a terse and extremely critical summation of the inquest.

"It wasn't satisfactory because they didn't allow full participation by the people most concerned, the Eskimos (Inuit) ... there were two and one-half Eskimos (Inuit) on board, counting the almost-born child.

They were not represented on the jury and they weren't

allowed to participate in the investigation through the Coroner by way of myself.

As a result, it is our view that a lot of real questions were never raised and a lot of answers just not forthcoming."

Karswick believed that, the technical approach to the whole inquest, "had the effect of restricting other parts of the investigation. These included factors of very real human interest relating to the medical care of the two patients, the famous suture being placed inside a woman who lived miles from civilization, and so on. With such a weight of technical evidence introduced during the inquest, you don't have an investigation, you just go through procedures," he charged.

10

"The aircraft had no special equipment," reported a government investigative team, "and the pilot had not been trained in the appropriate navigational technique. Consequently, it is not surprising that the pilot became lost when he attempted the flight into darkness and instrument flight conditions."

The 10-page report, compiled by the Ministry of Transport's Air Accident Investigation Division, was released in Ottawa on July 3, 1973.

It noted that Marten Hartwell, who began military flying training in Germany in 1944 and obtained a West German private pilot's license in 1958, qualified for a commercial pilot's license in December of 1967. This was followed by a multi-engine rating and night flying endorsement in December, 1970.

"Such qualifications permit a pilot to fly commercial flights with passengers under day VFR (Visual Flight Rules) conditions only," said the report.

It revealed that the lone survivor of the Arctic mercy flight had 2,085 hours total flying experience with 25 of these hours as pilot-in-command of the Beechcraft 18. There was also reference made to the trip attempted prior to the takeoff of the mercy flight.

"On the earlier flight that day, the pilot had disregarded his VFR restriction by entering cloud and he subsequently became uncertain of his position," said the report. "He had also disregarded the VFR restriction on previous occasions."

The basic findings of the report were that:

"The pilot undertook a flight involving flight in instrument conditions for which he was not qualified;

"The pilot had not been adequately trained for Arctic winter flying;

"The company did not adequately supervise its VFR (Visual Flight Rules) operation;

"The aircraft did not carry the survival equipment specified in Air Navigation Order Series V #12;

"The aircraft was not equipped for IFR or night flight in the area of compass unreliability;

"The existing standards for day VFR commercial aircraft operation do not take into account the winter Arctic conditions and consequently are routinely ignored."

The official government report, pointing out that Gateway Aviation was restricted to a "day VFR" operation, offered further criticism.

"On the flight to Cambridge Bay, the pilot climbed above cloud despite this restriction; similarly the flight that night was contrary to the provisions of the operating certificate. It was apparent to the investigators that these restrictions had been ignored on other occasions."

The report also criticized the lack of written instructions to the company's VFR pilots, which in effect, "left operational decisions up to the pilots which could be affected by the pay system (in this case a small base pay, a northern allowance, and mileage for completed revenue flights) based on mileage."

"The pilot's decision to accept the medical evacuation charter from Cambridge Bay to Yellowknife was made with the knowledge that night flight and flight through 'instrument weather' would be involved. His acceptance of the flight was no doubt related to the 'mercy' aspects but this cannot waive the 'day VFR' or the pilot's licensing restrictions."

Additionally, "the persons who engaged the charter displayed an unawareness of the restrictions under which the carrier operated and the hazards of the project flight," said the report.

The detailed findings, emphasizing the pilot's lack of appropriate navigational technique, also questioned his failure to make use of the knowledge he had.

"Because he made no enroute radio transmission to report that he was uncertain of his position," said the report, "he denied himself assistance from the ground and rendered more difficult the subsequent search and rescue operation."

"On the accident flight he displayed inadequate knowledge of the characteristics of the directional gyro, navigation techniques, the use of ADF (Automatic Direction Finder) equipment, radio communication procedures and the emergency locater transmitter."

There were additional findings:

"All non-directional radio beacons in the area of flight were operating normally as far as could be ascertained;

"The HF (high frequency) radio equipment operated by the company at Yellowknife was unserviceable;

"The survival equipment and supplies carried were inadequate in that there were no snowshoes and insufficient concentrated food;

"The emergency locater transmitter functioned properly. The instructions relating to the use of this equipment were not clear."

The condemning report was given widespread publicity by the Federal government. There was no explanation by the Ministry of Transport as to why it mailed the scathing document to many newsrooms throughout the nation (this is not normal procedure in the case of aircraft accident investigation) nor was there any explanation as to why the Ministry of Transport had not determined many of the abuses prior to the fatal crash.

Then Transport Minister Jean Marchand, quoted in a five

page prepared government news release, saw fit to explain it as best he could.

"Mr. Marchand noted that a number of points referred to in the investigators' findings were matters concerning which the Transport Ministry had been developing regulations or action programs as far back as two years," said the release, with an explanation that such a preparatory period is necessary in order to consult with industry.

There was also mention of the Minister's announcement in Yellowknife that followed the inquest.

"On March 17th, Mr. Marchand announced the issuance of a new Air Navigation Order, to become effective January 1, 1974, which establishes strict new standards for operation of small commercial aircraft, and also sets forth specific training requirements and proficiency requirements for flight crews and cabin attendants;

"During the Yellowknife visit, the Minister also referred to the continuing development of a $3.7 million program for expanding and improving air navigation facilities to meet both current and anticipated requirements in the Canadian Arctic;

"Referring to the final comment of the accident investigation report, that instructions relating to the use of the emergency locater transmitter were not clear, the Minister said that a new Air Navigation Order, which he announced in December, 1972, making ELTs (Emergency Locater Transmitters) mandatory for most Canadian aircraft, will also become effective January 1, 1974 ..."

The statements that followed the report were extremely interesting. The report had severely criticized pilot Marten Hartwell and Gateway Aviation for their errors. It was also evident, although not emphasized, that the Federal authorities had been extremely lax in enforcing current regulations. The Minister's remarks were encouraging but at the same time there were those who viewed them as a pacifier, coming far too late. Three people died and another almost succumbed and only now the Ministry of Transport was pledging to do something. The government agency's plain failure to enforce its regulations in the North was not followed by any mention of disciplinary action to be taken against those who should have spotted the irregularities long before the crash. But it was easy for the government. It covered its tracks by squarely placing the blame and then making a typical bureaucratic announcement that great changes were on the way. For Marten Hartwell and Gateway Aviation Limited, it would be much more difficult.

The survivor's license to pilot an aircraft had been suspended following the crash because he was assessed, "medically unfit."

Since then, Ministry officials have, "determined the pilot to be incompetent in flight navigation and in the use of the radio compass."

"Consequently, the pilot's license is now suspended until certain written examinations and a practical flight test have been successfully passed," stated the Federal government release.

"With respect to the company that employed the pilot," said the Ministry, "several operational audits and base inspections at Yellowknife, Edmonton, and Calgary have been completed by specialists from Ministry Headquarters and by regional officials."

Not making mention of where the "specialists" were in the months prior to the fatal flight, the statement continued, "as a result, a company operations manual has been approved; a new chief pilot responsible for the operational control of visual flight operations has been appointed; pilot training and flight proficiency checks have been brought up-to-date, and procedures instituted to ensure they will remain so; unauthorized instrument flight operations have been stopped; training programs and procedures have now been improved by the company to prevent inexperienced pilots acting as captains in flight conditions or over flight routes that are not authorized or are beyond their limits of training and experience."

"The investigation into the regulatory enforcement aspect is not yet complete on the company," warned the government. "Appropriate action will be taken if the evidence of the investigation warrants."

As expected, the Director of Operations for Gateway, Doug Rae, objected to the condemnation. Marten Hartwell remained silent.

GROUNDED — Hartwell as he appeared five years after the inquest. He did not remain grounded for long.

11

It was only nine days following release of the Ministry of Transport report that a $100,000 lawsuit was filed against Gateway Aviation and pilot Hartwell.

The statement of claim, issued in the courts of Alberta, charged negligence in the death of 27-year-old English nurse Judith Ann Hill. It claimed, "the crash would not have occurred if the defendants had exercised proper care in the maintenance, operation, and navigation of the aircraft."

Edmonton lawyer Philip Ketchum, acting on behalf of the young nurse's estate, quoted her father Lawrence (Jeffery) Hill as saying, "I don't want a penny for myself. Any monies recovered in this action will go directly to the Judith Hill Memorial Trust Fund to be used for the improvement and enhancement of nursing services and medical facilities in Canada's far North."

The statement of claim cited 12 examples of alleged negligence against the airline and pilot Hartwell.

"Flying the aircraft at an altitude that was unsafe under all the circumstances of the case including the terrain being flown over, the pilot's lack of familiarity with the terrain being flown over, and the adverse weather and light conditions limiting ground and forward visibility;

"Failing to keep a lookout, or in the alternative, any proper lookout;

"Failing to manoeuvre the aircraft so as to avoid flying it horizontally into the side of a hill;

"Flying the aircraft in northern latitudes when the pilot knew or ought to have known that darkness and adverse weather conditions would be encountered, and that he did not have sufficient experience and qualifications for such a flight;

"Failing to make regular enroute radio transmissions;

"Flying the aircraft within an area of compass unreliability without a means of establishing direction not dependent on a magnetic source, or in the alternative, in failing to use same;

"Flying the aircraft with faulty navigational and radio equipment;

"Failing to adequately maintain and inspect the navigational and radio equipment on the aircraft;

"Carrying passengers for reward in an aircraft flown by a pilot who had not been adequately trained for Arctic winter flying;

"Failing to adequately equip the aircraft for night flight and instrument flight in areas of compass unreliability when the defendants knew or ought to have known that such flights would be undertaken, and failing to adequately instruct their pilots on the use of such equipment, as was provided in the aircraft;

"Failing to adhere to the restrictions on the operation of the aircraft imposed by the Ministry of Transport, and failing to adequately supervise such operations and obtain clearances in emergency situations."

Lawyer Ketchum said the claim is for, "loss of expectation of life and the amenities of life."

He explained, "at the time of Judy's death, she had every prospect of enjoying many more years of a full, happy, successful, and rewarding life. With regard to the amount being claimed by the estate, the only thing I would say there is that a jury in Alberta recently awarded $90,000 to an exceptionally promising young man in the prime of life. My feeling is that

Miss Hill is certainly in a similar category."

The $90,000 award, according to the Edmonton lawyer, involved one of the most outstanding students at the University of Alberta. The youth was killed in a highway accident when a car apparently veered across the centre line of the road. Up until the award, which was appealed, the normal amount allocated by the courts under similar circumstances had been no higher than $10,000. It was particularly significant in that it wasn't a dependency claim, but rather a claim for, "just simply loss of expectation of life."

"The circumstances of the crash and the Ministry of Transport report speak for themselves," concluded the lawyer when asked to elaborate further on the $100,000 action against Gateway and pilot Hartwell.

In Fort Smith, NWT, Doug Rae, the Director of Operations for the airline said the company had been anticipating a legal suit.

"The insurance company will take it from here," he said. "We are fully covered. We are covered for a lot more than that."

Rae described the development as being, "like a doctor driving down the highway and taking the responsibility of trying to look after patients under conditions that are not ideal. Then they turn around and sue him ..."

Pilot Hartwell declined comment, but his lawyer Roy Henning, who was retained after Red Cavanagh's May appointment as an Alberta Court Judge, issued a brief statement. He said he had been served a copy of the statement of claim but had not read it yet.

"I'll read it in the morning," he said. "I can't say what kind of defence will be filed until I've read the statement, considered it, and discussed it with my client. He knows it was issued, but he hasn't read it either and has no comment."

In Toronto, lawyer James Karswick indicated another lawsuit was imminent.

"I have been instructed by the Eskimo (Inuit) Brotherhood to proceed with an action in the court of the Northwest Territories for compensation for the lives of the Eskimo (Inuit) passengers, Mrs. Neemee Nulliayok and David Kootook," he stated. "I have retained a lawyer in Inuvik to apply for letters of administration from the estate of the two deceased people."

Less than a month later action was taken.

A $205,000 lawsuit, termed legal dynamite, was filed against pilot Marten Hartwell and Gateway Aviation.

The statement of claim, placed in the courts of the Northwest Territories by lawyer Karswick, charged negligence and, "breach of contract to carry passengers safely."

The action was taken on behalf of the two Inuit passengers plus the unborn child, marking the first time in Canada that the estate of an unborn fetus had sued for, "loss of expectation of life," and the amenities of life.

The two-part triple action suit claimed compensation and damages of $50,000 for "loss of expectation of life" on behalf of the estate of David Kootook, and $40,000 under the Fatal Accidents Ordinance for his bereaved parents; $40,000 on behalf of the estate of Mrs. Neemee Nulliayok, and $50,000 as compensation for her bereaved husband and child.

The suit wound up with a precedent setting claim of $25,000 for loss of life on behalf of the estate of the unborn Nulliayok child, and for deprivation of the service of that child for the father.

The fetus had reached the 32-week or eighth month stage of gestation at the time of death. According to evidence introduced at the February inquest, the unborn child was a baby girl.

Among six examples of alleged negligence against Hartwell cited in the claim were: "undertaking a flight and operating an aircraft when he was not qualified, competent or experienced for the circumstances and conditions involved; flying too low, and failing to manoeuvre the aircraft so as to avoid flying it horizontally into the side of a hill."

The suit also gave four examples of alleged negligence by Gateway Aviation which, "caused or contributed to," the crash. These included, "failing to provide the services of a pilot who was properly trained and qualified in flying the aircraft under the conditions prevalent in the Northwest

Territories, and failing to provide an aircraft that was properly equipped with navigational, survival and flying aids."

In respect to the claims on behalf of the unborn baby and the bereaved father, the lawsuit brought with it the possibility of long-range implications.

"In law, there are very few authorities on the issue here," said Lawyer Karswick. "In Ontario, the only cases that have been decided upon, is where a child after birth, brings an action for injuries sustained while a fetus.

"Where we are going into a completely new area, is where an unborn child is never born, but dies as a result of injuries to the fetus, and whether it has the same status to bring action as a child born with the injuries. If you kill the fetus, do you take away that right?

"If you kill a woman as compared to a woman with a fetus," said Karswick, "there must be a difference. The loss must be greater. Should not the law recognize that?"

Karswick pointed out that if Mrs. Nulliayok had been carrying a camera aboard the plane, instead of a child, a claim could certainly have been made if that camera had been destroyed.

Canadian courts had not previously been called upon to render a definitive judgement as to the legal rights of the unborn fetus — or in fact, whether a fetus is an object or a person under the law.

Pro-life groups were quick to see the implications of the lawsuit.

"I think it is potential legal dynamite on both sides," said Dr. Heather Morris, President of Alliance for Life, a national co-ordinating pro-life group. "Whatever the final judgement, it will inevitably affect the rights of every unborn Canadian child."

Gwen Landolt, president of Right-to-Life, a Toronto pro-life group, agreed.

"The Canadian and English courts have consistently given more and more legal protection and recognition to the unborn child," she said. "It is hoped that it will continue to do so in this case." She concluded, "to do otherwise would be to turn its back on centuries of legal precedent, medical science and plain ordinary common sense."

12

Canadian theologians, asked to provide a moralist's viewpoint on the consumption of human flesh under certain circumstances, were not unanimous in their thinking. Regardless of the failure to reach unanimity, on a subject discussed among world churches, religious leaders generally came out with attitudes supporting the action taken by Marten Hartwell to sustain life.

Reverend Jean-Guy LeMarier, Dean of Theology at St. Paul's Roman Catholic Seminary in Ottawa said:

"In my opinion, there is no specific moral problem involved. In the tradition of Ethics and Moral Theology, cannibalism has never been, to my knowledge, an important issue. Incidental elements, like homicide or sexual perversion, have been studied and discussed, but the simple fact of eating human flesh has not been considered a moral dimension of the situation."

"The natural repugnance we feel is a sufficient check against expansion of the phenomenon," said Father LeMarier. "We should experiment deep understanding and compassion for our fellow men forced to resort to this unfortunate option."

One religious organization expressed complete opposition to the eating of human flesh under any circumstances. The views were put forward in a 1967 issue of The Watchtower, the official journal used by Jehovah's Witnesses around the world.

The article, pointing out that humans are allowed by God to eat animal flesh but not blood asks, "did this include eating human flesh, sustaining one's life by means of the body, or part of the body of another human, alive or dead?"

The answer is very clearly spelled out in the article. "No! That would be cannibalism, a practice abhorrent to all civilized people ...

"In allowing man to eat animal flesh, Jehovah God did not grant permission for humans to try to perpetuate their lives by cannibalistically taking into their bodies human flesh, whether chewed or in the form of whole organs or body parts taken from others."

Other churches, through their leaders, reacted differently. Archbishop E.W. Scott of the Anglican Church of Canada said, "compassion must be the guiding principle in any reflection of the tragic episode ... compassion for the survivor and for the relatives of the dead person or persons."

"There is a sense in which society has no right to judge this particular case," the Archbishop continued, "the event took place outside of society, beyond radio help, beyond communications beacons, and apparently beyond rescue."

"Driven only by the instinctive will to survive," added the church official, "Mr. Hartwell did what he did without violence to any living person and without malice towards himself."

The Primate of the Anglican Church of Canada, in offering his views on the moral aspect of consuming human flesh under certain circumstances, also criticized the news media.

"A larger, and more critical issue," he said, "is the sensational reporting and the stirring up of human feelings by the media on one hand, and the kind of morbid curiosity which many persons have revealed on the other ... Some of the media reporting (in all three of the mass media — newspapers, radio, and television), was guilty of sensationalism that added nothing to our knowledge and played on the negative side of human curiosity."

The President of the Maritime Conference of the United

Church of Canada also expressed an opinion on the action taken by the pilot.

"I think it is wrong for anyone to be judgmental about Marten Hartwell's alleged eating of human flesh," stated Reverend Willard C. Picketts, "for no one knows what they would do under similar circumstances."

"One would have to be in that situation," stated Reverend Picketts, "lonely, freezing, starving, with human flesh that might support life until rescue could come, before they could say what they would do."

Citing, "situational ethics," Reverend Picketts added, "as much as it may be repugnant to the individual mind at the thought of eating human flesh, there is really nothing morally wrong with it on religious grounds."

The tragedy and the revelation that human flesh had been eaten resulted in many, many opinions being expressed by the general public. A random sampling included comments such as:

"It makes me sick thinking about it. I wouldn't have done it."

"I never really had thought of such a thing. If it hadn't been for the Andes story and now this one, I doubt if I would have even considered it."

"Your life is the most precious thing you have. You should do everything possible to preserve it."

"I wouldn't have liked it, but I think I would have done it."

"Who am I to judge? Who knows what can happen under such circumstances?"

Public support for Hartwell was also evident in numerous letters published in various newspapers. Editorials, including one published in the *Toronto Sun*, also took a clear-cut stand.

The Marten Hartwell inquest in Yellowknife is now history, but the unsavory details of the case still linger on.

The Sun was the first Canadian newspaper to reveal the cannibalism aspects, so it is perhaps understandable that we should draw a certain amount of reaction. We didn't comment editorially earlier because it seemed obvious and acceptable that a person should eat human flesh in order to survive.

Extraordinarily, some people disagree in the most extreme terms, some even scold the *Sun* for mentioning cannibalism at all, much less for making a big (perhaps too big) play over it.

First of all we think it is a tribute to the human will that a person can force himself to eat human flesh in order to survive. We have nothing but sympathy and admiration for Hartwell in being strong enough to force himself to do it. Those Paraguayan footballers who crashed and ate their dead companions compared it to a heart transplant — the using of dead body parts to keep their bodies alive. It is an apt analogy.

Surely society has progressed since the 1840's when one Lewis Keseberg was hounded and vilified for the remainder of his life after he survived by eating starved members of the Donner party which was trapped by winter in the Rockies!

The main reason such a fuss was made by the media over the Hartwell business was because such a curtain of secrecy and mystery was officially lowered over the plane crash. This, not the deed itself or the press reaction, was the disservice to Hartwell — and to truth and the abstract of information.

It was almost a conspiracy of silence. Small wonder that certain officials felt unnatural and uneasy over such undemocratic restrictions, and therefore talked — off the record.

Hartwell has suffered enough. But he should not torture himself because he ate human flesh. It is our hope that were we in a similar situation, we too would find the courage to stay alive by eating the dead. And, were we among the victims, we would hope others would stay alive by consuming us.

Let that be the last word on the matter.

13

The Marten Hartwell story, as its main character, refused to die. It remained implanted in the minds of those around the world who were given a steady flow of information, long after it began. Innumerable, varied developments have transpired in the years that have intervened.

First, the Armed Forces announced that one of its members, Warrant Officer H.J. (Bud) Howells, had invented a spotter's box that would increase the efficiency of searchers by as much as 60 per cent.

Howells came up with the idea, a module constructed of plywood and plexi-glass that can be fastened to the tail of a plane's cargo ramp within minutes, after he went to a Christmas party. He explained, "a lady jumped me and demanded, why aren't you doing something to help these people?"

She told him, "I could do the job in a telephone booth."

During the search for the mercy flight, with spotters strapped to the loading ramps of the search aircraft, the wind chill factor was at times 100 degrees below zero fahrenheit.

Next, searchmaster Keith Gathercole and his assistant, Trevor White, received the Order of Military Merit.

Afterwards, Red Cavanagh was not the only lawyer involved in the case to be sworn-in as a judge. Howard Irving, James

Karswick, Philip Ketchum and William Trainor were all appointed to the Bench. Mr. Justice Cavanagh, described as a top criminal law expert, died after a long bout with respiratory problems in mid-January, 1991. The former flying officer in World War II was just months shy of mandatory retirement on his 75th birthday.

Inspector Tom Venner was appointed a Divisional Intelligence Officer with the RCMP, overseeing the collection of criminal data as it related to organized crime.

He later became Commanding Officer of the RCMP 'E Division', covering all of the province of British Columbia, prior to his retirement as a Deputy Commissioner of the force.

Walter England was again called upon as Coroner to investigate yet another Arctic wilderness crash. Thirty-two people aboard a Panarctic aircraft, perished near Rea Point. One of the victims, an Inuit, was returning home after receiving medical attention in a hospital outside the Territories.

The unfolding events were endless.

Northern nurses sought danger pay, and in two instances, refused to fly as escorts.

The nurses in the Northwest Territories established a Memorial Fund to commemorate Judy Hill and nurse Julia May King who was killed in a crash in April, 1968.

Philip Ketchum announced the Judy Hill Memorial Fund.

The charitable foundation, which began with an out-of-court settlement of the $100,000 lawsuit filed against Gateway Aviation and pilot Hartwell, distributed nearly $80,000 in scholarships by its 15th anniversary. At that time, the fund contained a balance of $65,000.

The educational trust, which accepts all contributions, is designed to enable nurses to improve their qualifications for service in the Arctic. A similar fund in the United Kingdom, which has since merged with its Canadian counterpart, also attained a good response.

Those who are interested in contributing or learning more about the program can make known their views by corresponding to:

The Judy Hill Memorial Fund
15325 Whitemud Road
Edmonton, Alberta, Canada
T6H 4N5
Telephone (403) 434-6022.

The parents and brother of Judy Hill, among the first to contribute to the plan which also received a $25,000 donation from the Federal government, visited the tiny Inuit settlement of Spence Bay several months after the ill-fated emergency mission. Sadly, Judy Hill's last letter to her parents, written on the day of her final flight, related that she was beginning to wrap Christmas presents for her family.

That December, her mother boarded an aircraft in England for a journey to attend the burial service and subsequent cremation of her daughter. The casket was closed.

Nurse Hill, nicknamed 'Angel of the Snow' by a newspaper, later was the subject of a book by the same name. The publication, said to have received limited circulation due to matters of copyright, followed a British Broadcasting Corporation (BBC) documentary entitled, 'The Angel'.

Judy Hill's father, Jeffery who was an engineer by profession, died in 1980.

Her mother, Eda who was a registered nurse, died in 1988.

Timothy, Judy's brother, continued to reside in England.

David Kootook was not forgotten either, although the public memory of him soon faded.

Buried in a graveside service attended by only two individuals other than the Minister, he was nominated for the Commissioner's Award for Bravery in the Northwest Territories. He was also recommended by several people for the Governor-General's Award for Bravery.

When the Federal award had not been granted more than a year after the crash, David Ward who was then an Edmonton Alderman, wrote the Governor-General probing the reason for the delay.

"Is it because of his age, sex, or racial background?" queried

Ward.

It was also Ward, an Inuit who now practices law, who demanded that the City of Edmonton properly mark the boy's grave.

Two years after the youngster's death, the burial plot had still not been properly signed. Ward, then took it upon himself to, in his words, "ensure that a marker was placed."

His efforts took more than two additional years. It was not until the spring of 1977, more than four years after David lost his life, that the simple, flat marker was installed.

It tells scant little about the young hero whose burial place is in north Edmonton's Beechmount cemetery. The stark reminder reads:

DAVID KOOTOOK

August 13, 1958   December, 1972

David Ward describes the Inuit as, "the forgotten people." In the case of the young hero, Ward was the most vocal of the too few who seemed to remember.

That same elected Municipal official announced that more than $6,000, which he had raised, was being donated to establish a library in memory of the youngster in the Northwest Territories. It was a dream of Ward's that disappointingly never came true. Instead, the money initially was used to purchase audio-visual equipment. More recently, according to library officials, donations have been used to buy reference material for children.

Although there is no David Kootook library, nor for that matter is there even a photograph of him, donations are still being accepted in care of:

The David Kootook Memorial Fund
NWT Public Library Services
Post Office Box 1100
Hay River, Northwest Territories, Canada
X0E 0R0

The lawsuit that was filed on behalf of the Inuit victims was resolved for an undisclosed sum described by one lawyer as, "sizeable." The fact that the issue was settled out-of-court meant that there was no precedent established in relation to the claim for damages in the death of the unborn fetus.

The issue was not settled until 1991. In an unrelated case, the Supreme Court of Canada ruled that a fetus cannot be considered a person. It upheld a decision by the British Columbia Court of Appeal that found an unborn child cannot be considered a person until it has completely left its mother's body.

Support continued to grow for Marten Hartwell.

Juror Rocky Parsons of Yellowknife was one of many to write letters to newspapers.

"We were so busy affixing blame," said Parsons, "I forgot to say 'welcome back' and as a former member of the jury would like to set the record straight."

There was, then Transport Minister Jean Marchand, promising in Yellowknife that $4 million would be allocated for expanding and upgrading navigational facilities in the Arctic.

It was Marchand, earlier asked to comment on the suspension of Hartwell's flying license by the Ministry of Transport, who told a questioner in the House of Commons, "we will see when he is recovered if he still can pilot a plane."

As far as the pilot's future with Gateway Aviation, it did not look good.

"I'll wait until he's ready to fly and when he comes in to see me, I'll see," said Operations Manager Doug Rae. "I don't think it would be a good move on his part. If he has another accident, especially in bush flying, they'll just be on top of him."

Rae added, "If I put myself in his position, if I was him, I'd blow the country. He's had offers of jobs."

Gateway Aviation later went out of business.

In mid-August, Hartwell travelled with his girlfriend to Yellowknife to pick up personal belongings left in the community immediately following his rescue. Clean shaven and requesting that photographs not be taken, he told reporters that he would like to fly again in the North because of the challenges. Conceding the possibility that his pilot's license would never be returned, he hinted that he may take up farming in Canada. His father had farmed in Germany.

It was only a few days subsequent that the RCMP closed the file on the case. Investigating officers, who had returned to the crash scene, failed to come up with any further evidence including the second ration box that has never been found. The scattered wreckage remained, although it appeared as though some sightseers, or the morbidly curious, had visited the remote area.

The man whose wife, Emmy, described as, "only happy when in a plane", contemplated a return to northern flying, but it remained uncertain. He could simply decide to change locale. Australia, for example, was very much in need of bush pilots.

In the meantime, Hartwell continued living in the one-bedroom apartment that he shared with Susan Haley.

Compensation from the insurance company, at about two-thirds or three-quarters of his normal pay, assisted in meeting the $127 monthly rent. Previously, the two occupants had been used to a pilot's monthly base rate of $550 plus eight cents a mile for every mile flown. Assuredly, there had been an incentive to fly as many miles as possible.

The walk-up apartment in south Edmonton's university area had proven a relatively secure place for Hartwell and his friend, both preferring to keep their affairs private.

Their neighbors appreciated the feelings of the couple living in suite number 26.

Lucille Korpan remembered seeing Hartwell two or three times.

"You would say that he was a normal, quiet man, and being there was so much publicity, I felt that he'd like his neighbors to leave him alone," she said.

Glenn Wolochatiuk knew his neighbor only as a man with a beard and a crutch.

"I thought he looked like a gloomy person," he recalled,

"our eyes met for a second and then he was gone."

It was in this apartment that Hartwell gave his statement to the RCMP. It was from here where he heard the many new twists in his continuing story, and waited patiently for the daily return of his girlfriend from the nearby campus. From this supposedly secret hideaway, listed in the telephone book in the name of a former roommate of Susan Haley, until her boyfriend moved in, the survivor constantly communicated with his lawyer.

One of the decisions made following the crash was to sell his exclusive story to the Observer newspaper in London, England.

"The value (from an original offer of $25,000) went down quite a bit after the inquest," stated lawyer Cavanagh. But there were royalties, he continued, "how do you think he is going to pay me?"

Even though both Hartwell and Miss Haley consistently decried the amount of publicity given the story, they did agree to sell it. One of the reasons they chose, other than the money, is because Miss Haley thought the newspaper would handle it tastefully.

It was strange, as the mass circulation daily that they selected is widely known for its belief in the news view of Lord Northcliffe. The British publishing tycoon's definition is straightforward, "News is something that someone, somewhere is trying to suppress — all the rest is advertising."

Surprisingly enough, even after the deal with the British newspaper had been worked out and it was learned that the couple was planning on further publicizing the saga by writing a book, Hartwell said, "I've had enough of this whole story and in my opinion it should not be published any more." He maintained that he wanted to put his memories behind him, yet the rights to the Observer allowed it to market his story in serial form to other newspapers around the world. In addition, Hartwell granted an interview to Canada's weekly newsmagazine, MacLean's.

In the beginning, when first rescued and offers came in, he said that if he sold the story the income would be shared with the families of the victims. None of the relatives, according to their legal counsel, were advised of any monies being donated.

Public opinion, a fickle thing at best, changed.

At first, staunchly in defence of the man whose living nightmare was front page news for days on end, feeling that he should be left in privacy, many were now puzzled by the pilot's interview and forthcoming willing adventure into print.

During a telephone conversation with me following the inquest, Hartwell's initial words were somewhat unexpected.

"I have been starving for your call," he said, and then explained that he was expecting to hear from me.

His slightly accented voice, which was rather quiet, sounded mixed with curiosity and relief.

"I just came back from the dentist and wasn't involved with anything," said the pilot, "so you got me at a good time."

He talked about numerous aspects of his tribulations during the lengthy conversation.

He wondered aloud if he should stay in Canada, saying that he was more well-known than U-S President Richard Nixon, and if he goes anywhere, not only the adults but the children know him as well.

Hartwell talked about the lack of protection for pilots in situations like he was in and questioned what his tragic experience would mean for pilots faced with mercy flights in the future.

"You can take any bush pilot's word and take my word and it will be the same," said Hartwell. "As a bush pilot you work 24 hours a day and get six or seven hours paid for, and once anyone has an accident you're condemned."

He seemed extremely curious about public reaction to all of the news stories that had been reported about his ordeal.

"I got letters from all over the world," he said, "most of them congratulated me and so on."

He made reference to the parents of Judy Hill, the young nurse with whom he had indulged in necrophageous activity.

"If they would not have heard anything about it, it certainly would have been much better," he stated. "They sent me flowers."

Not once during the conversation did Hartwell appear to be upset. But despite his confident voice it was all too evident that the days of horror weighed heavily upon his mind.

"Sometimes I was almost ready to get a rope, and I don't want to be bothered by anyone," he said. "I want to have a little privacy too — I want the people to forget and I want to be a private man again."

Perhaps the most memorable quote attributed to Hartwell is the one contained in his statement to the police. It is worth repeating.

"I think it is clear to the authorities what I did, and I won't go through the emotional side of the experience once again," he stated. "I am still trying to forget this and probably will never succeed."

Neither would the relatives of the dead. But for those who still question, for those who still doubt, one can only ask — IN THE SAME CIRCUMSTANCES, WHAT WOULD YOU HAVE DONE?

DEEP CONVERSATION — The survivor conversing with an unidentified female in the lobby of the building that contained his lawyer's offices.

REACTION — The media wanted
more which proved upsetting.

14

"It has always been among all social levels of all people," stated Bradford Angier in his book HOW TO STAY ALIVE IN THE WOODS, "that famishing human beings left to their own resources will devour anything even suspected of having food value, and eventually will resort to cannibalism."

There are a number of examples, going back in history, where hunger has led to the eating of human flesh.

"In the last century the crew of the American Whaler Essex, lost in the Atlantic, ate each other almost to the last man," said Cord Christian Troebst in the ART OF SURVIVAL.

The writing continued, "during the two world wars there were cases where the occupants of lifeboats, although they did not kill each other for food, did eat the limbs of their fellows who had died a natural death."

Troebst also tells of a case in 1948 at Foxe Basin where an Inuit woman and her daughter ate the bodies of the husband and father and son.

History is replete with stories where human flesh has been used to sustain life.

Guy Blanchet related in his book, SEARCH IN THE NORTH, the case of a young Inuit girl at Chesterfield who survived the strong taboo against cannibalism held by the Inuit. He tells how it was necessary for the girl to be given police protection because she was regarded with horror and became an outcast among her own people.

Polar explorer and author Peter Freuchen, related the tale of an Inuit woman who killed four of her five starving children.

The story of the Donner party, which unravelled in the 1840's, has become part of the American frontier legend. Lewis Keseberg, a tall, handsome German who had emigrated to America only two years before the tragic wagon train journey, was injured and left behind with a woman when the travellers, lost in deep snow, set off for help.

He later told rescuers that the woman died after about a week and when his provisions gave out, it was four days before he could taste human flesh. He claims it was that or death.

He is quoted as saying, "the flesh of starved beings contains little nutriment. It is like feeding straw to horses. I can not describe the unutterable repugnance with which I tasted the first mouthful of flesh.

"There is an instinct in our nature that revolts at the thought of touching, much less eating, a corpse. This food was never otherwise than loathsome, insipid and disgusting. For nearly two months I was alone in that dismal cabin. No one knows what occurred but myself, no living being ever before was told of the occurrences."

Keseberg, who said he boiled the flesh added, "God Almighty had provided only this one horrible way for me to subsist. The necessary mutilation of the bodies of those who had been my friends, rendered the ghastliness of my situation more frightful."

When rescuers reached Keseberg, the sight was beyond comprehension.

According to one of the rescuers, Captain R.P. Tucker, "human bodies, terribly mutilated legs, arms, skulls, and portions of remains were scattered in every direction and strewn about the camp."

The body of one of the women was found with one of her

limbs sawed off. The saw was near her remains.

Captain Tucker wrote, "the dead bodies lay mouldering around, being all that was left to tell the tale of sorrow."

A newspaperman and sometimes politician, Charles McGlashan, began working on a story 37 years after the Donner party tragedy.

He related how Keseberg, throughout the remainder of his life, was faced with business reverses, the death of his wife, and two hopelessly idiotic children remaining at home. The children screamed so loudly that the family could not live near other people.

Said McGlashan, here he lives, the saddest, loneliest, most pitiable creature on the face of the earth. He traces all his misfortunes to that cabin on Donner Lake, and it is little wonder that he says: "I beg of you, insert in your book (HISTORY OF THE DONNER PARTY: A TRAGEDY OF THE SIERRA) a fervent prayer to Almighty God that he will forever prevent the recurrence of a similar scene of horror."

It was not that many years later, in 1904, that one of the Eastern Arctic's most well known tales unfolded. It was first recorded by Knud Rasmussen, carefully researched by Father Guy Marie Rousseliere, O.M.I., and written about by Ray Price in the book HOWLING ARCTIC: THE REMARKABLE PEOPLE WHO MADE CANADA SOVEREIGN IN THE FARTHEST NORTH. Several pages are devoted to Monica Ataguttaaluk.

The story surrounds a famine in the early 1900's on Baffin Island, when a small group of Pond Inlet Inuit moved deep into the interior to hunt for caribou. The hunt was unsuccessful, but when some members of the party returned, three Inuit and their families remained behind. The book relates how the families starved. They ate everything and then the bodies of the dead. An Inuit woman, when found in the midst of human bones and entrails after eating her husband and children, was faced with loneliness, hunger and fear. She was taken by her rescuers back to Igloolik where she lived until 1948, becoming famous in the North.

THE SURVIVOR

Years later, there would be another story of cannibalism to gain worldwide attention. It was called by some, 'The Christmas Miracle' and hit the international spotlight in December, 1972. The saga, in the snow capped Andes of South America, began two months earlier when a Uruguayan plane carrying 45 persons slammed into a mountain peak. The F-27 turboprop, with a crew of five, was on a two and one-half hour flight from Montevideo to Santiago. Aboard were 16 members of a rugby team and 24 friends and relatives. Without warning, the plane hit the icy peak and the lives of many were snuffed out. Eighteen were dead or dying. The survivors huddled together and were able to learn through a transistor radio hooked up to a battery that a search had begun. Eight days later, they learned that it had been abandoned until the spring thaw, vanishing hopes for a quick rescue. For more than two months the survivors fought cold and starvation, with many slowly dying. Every day was a tragedy. An avalanche buried more of the survivors, resulting in added death. Others died of injury or starvation. Those who lived, learned again by radio, that the search had been resumed, but by now they were making other plans for rescue. Three of the survivors took off down the mountain for help. One of them later returned when it was decided it would make the food supply for the other two that much greater. On December 20th, the two haggard looking survivors were spotted by a Chilean shepherd, but they were still some distance away. He thought they were beggars and shouted that they could spend the night where they were and he would return the next day. The next morning the rescue began. Sixteen had survived. They told reporters that they had rationed chocolate bars, cheese, and lichen broth and melted snow for drinking water. Officials who had not seen the crash scene were astonished. The survivors had suffered great weight losses but could still walk. They were also remarkably mentally alert.

The mountain rescue team knew differently than those who had not seen the isolated area where the wreckage of the craft was strewn.

They discovered bodies near the wreck that had been carved and mutilated in a manner unrelated to a plane crash. Human limbs were found scattered outside the craft. Pieces of human flesh were hanging inside. The group had cut off parts of the body by using razor blades. An axe was also used. Sections of the dead bodies had been thawed on the warm metal of the aircraft, but eaten raw because there was no fuel for a fire. The bodies were not those of relatives nor were they ones with injuries that may have been infected. A rationing system was also apparently established with each corpse to last the group five days.

The survivors, all men, had lasted for over 70 days in deep snow and sub-zero temperatures. They lived only because they took extremely grim measures. They had eaten the flesh of their own. They had survived the Cordillera which had a reputation of never giving anyone back. Some of the survivors, later speaking of the hideousness that had taken place, likened the cannibalism to a heart transplant and claimed it would have been suicide to have acted differently.

A priest was quoted in a Santiago newspaper as saying," the body must have a fitting place, and in the case of the dead of the Uruguayan aircraft, this place was to serve as food for survivors."

Another priest told a Thanksgiving mass held for the survivors, "what happens to them will depend on us now, and on the love and understanding that we are capable of giving them."

And it was a Chilean newspaper that carried a headline, CANNABALISM JUSTIFIED, followed by another headline with the subtitle, WHAT WOULD YOU HAVE DONE?

While the 16 young Uruguayans were eating the flesh of their dead companions on that icy ledge in the Chilean mountains, Marten Hartwell was forced to make that same agonizing decision alone, thousands of miles away.

Neither Hartwell, nor young David Kootook, who finally perished after struggling against death for 23 days, were the first, nor will they be the last to suffer the agony inflicted by the cruelty of the northern lands.

The longest modern record of survival in the Northwest Territories occurred in 1961 when two Yellowknife prospectors fought starvation for more than two months in the Nahanni valley. The prospectors, Dean Rossworn and John Richardson, were scheduled to be taken out of the area in March, but their plane failed to arrive. Finally rescued in May, they told of a meagre diet that consisted of boiled caribou hide and tree bark. They had also eaten six dogs and made soup by boiling the bones of the animals.

A 47-year-old Edmonton man is believed to have lived for 52 days following the crash of his aircraft in January 1962. Although Blake MacKenzie was never found, a diary he had written indicated he had lived for that length of time.

For a full 49 tortured days (February 4 to March 25, 1963), 42-year-old Ralph Flores of San Bruno, California and 21-year-old Helen Klaben of Brooklyn, New York, waged a daily battle against the perils of the northern wilderness and won. The Flores plane, blown off course in snow and fog, plummeted into a heavily wooded mountain area about 80 miles southeast of Watson Lake in the Yukon. When rescued they told of melting snow for water, pretending it was soup, and trying unsuccessfully to catch rabbits. Miss Klaben was suffering gangrene in a broken right foot (the toes later had to be amputated), frostbite to both heels, and a broken left arm. The pilot had smashed ribs, two frostbitten toes, a broken jaw, and an ugly gash across his lips and chin which had bled for days after the plane had gone down. Both miraculously escaped another of the North's harrowing tales of disappearance that so often had meant soundless death. It was estimated that Miss Klaben, who lost 45 pounds, could have lasted another week and the pilot, who had lost over 50 pounds, another four days. The will to survive, the amount of activity undertaken during such conditions, a person's emotional state, and energy necessary to maintain body temperature, were all cited as contributing factors to the survival. It was a story that later was the subject of a U.S. network television movie, featuring

Edward Asner and Sally Struthers.

Over the years, history has recorded numerous cases of those being lost in the wilderness.

Prospector Jim Barton of Snow Lake, Manitoba went without solid food for a full 50 days after a misunderstanding resulted in him not being picked up from a summer camp in the Yukon. Rescued at the end of October 1966, Barton told how he had remained in his sleeping bag holding snow close to his body so it would melt for drinking water. When rescued his feet were badly frozen.

One of the most phenominal stories about man's will to live unfolded on April 1, 1967. Thirty-nine-year-old Robert Gauchie was rescued after being imprisoned in the sub-Arctic for 58 days. Gauchie, who endured record 50-below zero temperatures and a wind chill factor down to 90-below, had been on a flight from Cambridge Bay to Yellowknife when he encountered a severe snowstorm south of Contwoyto. He was alone in the plane carrying a cargo of fish. When rescued, Gauchie who lost 54 pounds, told how he had survived by consuming eight pounds of concentrated ration and the arctic char that was part of the cargo.

"All I can say is that Hartwell did not display much self-discipline," stated Sheldon Coleman, "and at the expense of sounding 'corny', did not uphold the tradition of the early northern pilots and crew."

Coleman's opinion can be well taken. The RCAF Flight Lieutenant, along with Joseph Fortey, survived 31 days after their plane was forced down on the northwest slope of Point Lake, about 250 miles northwest of Fort Reliance, Northwest Territories. It occurred during a thunderstorm on August 17, 1936. Aboard the craft was one emergency ration kit designed to last one man for 14 days. Besides this, both men consumed two ground squirrels and some blueberries. When rescued, Flight Lieutenant Coleman had lost 20 pounds while his companion Aircraftsman Fortey's weight had dropped 30 pounds. Neither had suffered injury when the plane was forced down. Upon their rescue, doctors said both would only have lasted about another week and Coleman agreed, "if it had turned cold I imagine about a week, unless one of us got a chill."

There are countless stories of men surviving inhumane conditions in the frozen North, and elsewhere. Pilot Alf Caywood and Air Mechanic Jack Rennie were brought out alive after nine days and nights of 40-below zero temperatures in the Barren Lands. Their gruelling adventure began when their plane burst into flame while in flight. A passenger burned to death, but Caywood and Rennie, without solid food, miraculously lived through the long, lonely hours spent in the Arctic cold during the early part of 1942.

Troebst tells of 23-year-old Flight Lieutenant David Steeves, who ejected from a jet over the Sierra Nevada in May, 1957. He twisted both ankles, but despite this handicap, managed to walk 100 miles to his rescue within 54 days. He lost 40 pounds during the ordeal.

Troebst also tells of two members of a crew who bailed out over Newfoundland by mistake. One of the men was injured, but the other loaded him onto his shoulders and headed southward through the snow. During the next 48 days, with the other man still on his shoulders, he covered 150 miles until he finally reached safety. In another case, also related by Troebst, a pilot left his wrecked plane during an Arctic winter and came upon the huts (food store) of Arctic hunters. Eighty-four days later he was found by a group of Inuit who led him back to civilization.

It was no more remarkable than the case of 24-year-old Lieutenant Leon Crane of the United States Airforce, who was lost for 84 days in the frozen wilds of Alaska. With temperatures down to about 30 or 40-below zero Fahrenheit, Crane walked for more than 100 miles through ice and snow before reaching safety. The drama was revealed in March, 1944.

Some two years later, two Wisconsin men trekked 150 miles through the wilderness when their plane crashed in northern Alberta. They were lost for nearly three weeks in the bitter cold. A few months later flight Lieutenant Bill McKenzie of

Winnipeg, survived a 26-day solitary ordeal in the northern wilds after flying his jet propelled aircraft into a small wilderness lake. For 23 of the hopeless 26 days and nights, McKenzie had nothing to eat and lost 40 pounds. He lived on water. It was following his rescue that doctors estimated that McKenzie could have lived from 50 to 60 days without food provided he had lots of water and did not over exert himself.

There are numberless stories of people missing for various lengths of time in the North and living to tell the tale. Two haggard, exhausted men spent 10 days without food during a 20-day ordeal on a flight north of Edmonton; five men survived 12 days in the crash of a U.S. Navy plane in the wilds of northeastern Saskatchewan, and a 26-year-old flyer walked 75 miles for help after parachuting from his plane that ran out of fuel. Two Wisconsin sportsmen, marooned for nearly three weeks in Canada's far North, were rescued after a time of hunger, insects, cold and despair. They told rescuers they were almost killed by black flies.

There is the case of four men dramatically rescued after 37 days in the wilderness of Quebec; three persons who survived an almost three week long ordeal when the floats of their plane crashed through an ice covered lake, and many others who survived after being left in wastelands for varying periods up to two weeks.

There is the tale of horror from Rio De Janeiro, where six survivors of a Brazilian plane crash watched the buzzards prey above them. They fed on ants, grasshoppers, and termites. It was only a few months later that a diary told how a dying family of three existed on snow for an agonizing, two months. Their plane had crashed in mountains near Redding, California. The diary was found near the bones of the dead.

A nine year old boy, who chewed roots and leaves and drank rain water, was rescued after 15 days of hunger following a plane crash in northern Manitoba.

The boy, Walter Sedor, had followed his dying father's advice and stayed by the plane.

In Quebec, three years later, two men walked 60 miles

through the Arctic cold to end one of the country's largest air searches. The trek was made in 20-below zero Fahrenheit weather and resulted in the rescue of all aboard a downed Norseman aircraft.

In 1969, a Roman Catholic priest was rescued in British Columbia following a plane crash that left him stranded and without proper meals for 23 days. Reverend Emil Sasges walked almost 40 rugged miles before he was found. He lost 40 pounds during the ordeal.

There is the case of an Alaskan flier, prospector and trapper who walked 75 miles through the northern bushlands for help, and a 47-year-old pilot missing for 18 days in 40-below weather. He was found by an Inuit after walking for two weeks through the snow. The number of heroical survival tales are endless. A foodless walk for 60 miles in temperatures of 70-below; the case of a 17-year-old girl who survived an airplane crash in the Peruvian jungle and was found semi-conscious after wandering for days, and a 117-day fight to survive at sea. Forty-one-year-old Maurice Bailey and his 32-year-old wife Marilyn were emaciated but ecstatic when rescued. They survived by eating sharks, turtles, and seagulls, and drinking rainwater.

And so the pain and suffering endured by Marten Hartwell and the tremendous will to live that he exhibited, is by no means unique. Neither is the choice he made to ensure survival.

The decision he made, is the correct one as far as experts weighing the practicality of such drastic steps are concerned.

"Although it is true that under ideal conditions the human body can sometimes fend off starvation for upwards of two months by living on its own tissues," states Bradford Angier in his book HOW TO STAY ALIVE IN THE WOODS ... "It is equally certain that such auto-cannibalism is seldom necessary in the North American wilderness."

Angier continues, "a good rule is not to pass up any reasonable food sources if we are ever in need. There are many dead men who, through ignorance or fastidiousness, died."

The same theory is advanced by Major Dick Connick, then

Commanding Officer of the Canadian Forces Survival Training School at Canadian Forces Base Edmonton.

"The eating of human flesh isn't mentioned," said Connick, "but the men are told that anything that flies, crawls, swims, or walks is edible."

While the first essential to northern survival is the will to live, there are also certain ground-rules that should be followed.

The 49-year-old Connick, a former RCMP member who was stationed in the Arctic said, "we teach our men that if there are emergency rations they shouldn't be used until all other methods of living off the land have been exhausted."

Gateway official Doug Rae also provided some enlightening observations on survival in the North.

"With no food you can live for 14 days as long as you have a little over two quarts of water a day," said Rae. "A person should try not to eat for two days as it shrinks up your stomach. Then the rations are just for survival. You can live for a hell of a long time if you use your head."

Rae, specifically asked if he would find it a problem to survive for a month under the same conditions facing the German pilot replied, "I wouldn't say there wouldn't be any problem but if you know what you're doing you can do it."

"I told him previously that if he's down he should rip off an airplane tire and set it on fire," added the Gateway man. "It's easy to look back but if this had been done they would have found him much sooner, probably within 10 to 14 days which is the usual search period."

According to survival experts, and again according to Cord Troebst, it is possible to go for up to 60 days without food.

EPILOGUE

Two years following the crash, a Ministry of Transport official divulged that there had been no flight regulation changes directly attributable to the Hartwell experience.

Two years, almost to the day of the crash, a veteran member of the military termed the Armed Forces emergency disaster plan for Arctic flights, "a disaster in itself." He was commenting on word that a scheme had been devised to guard against the possibility of needless victims should a jumbo jet crash along any of the polar routes. It was developed due to a tremendous increase in the use of such airspace by major airlines.

The longtime Airforce officer called the plan "ridiculous and useless" because "there hasn't been enough money put aside for either proper training or equipment." He told me that if all aboard a Panarctic Oil company plane that crashed in the High Arctic had survived (all perished) the Armed Forces would have been powerless to save them. He claimed there would barely be enough equipment for rescuers and even if they did drop near the crash site there were no long-range helicopters to remove any who might have lived. He declared that para-rescue crews could only comfort those at a major disaster location in the North. "With an equipment shortage and lack of proper helicopters," he gave notice, "people would end up dying anyhow."

Five years from the time of the inquest, the Coroners Ordinance of the Northwest Territories was amended. It removed discrimination on the basis of sex that was raised during the inquiry as being contrary to the Canadian Bill of Rights. It would ensure that future jury members would consist of "six persons" rather than "six male members."

Amendments to the Coroners Act, published in 1988, show that lawyers representing "persons with an interest" now have the right to participate at inquests. It allows them to call, examine and cross-examine witnesses. It marked a great departure from the proceedings of 1972 when such involvement was denied all legal counsel with the exception of the Crown agent.

Almost two decades after the crash, in respect to compelling witnesses to attend and testify at Coroner inquests in the Territories, the regulations continued to remain unchanged. If they depart the region, as Hartwell who was the only living eyewitness did, there is no law forcing them to return and face questions under oath. The situation is similar throughout the nation.

Insofar as implementing the jury majority and minority recommendations, all but one is in effect. "Most of the credit goes to advancements in technology and the passage of time — not the MOT", according to former jury member Robert O'Connor. He is disappointed, however, that one of his key recommendations remains outstanding.

He believed strongly — and still does — that the words, "check your ELT (Emergency Locater Transmitter) armed", follow final communications between airport towers or air-radio facilities and aircraft departing on all across Canada flights.

The Transport Department has failed to make such a check mandatory and O'Connor was disturbed at the reluctance on the part of the federal agency to take action, "especially with the big drive for aviation safety."

An MOT official claimed that a reminder of the equipment is part of a pilot's checklist and that is good enough. The founder of Aero Arctic and proponent of the idea disagreed, "it is only a few words, why not?" questioned O'Connor who is still active in northern flying.

Also in early 1991, former juror O'Connor warned of a "glaring deficiency not addressed" in connection with downed aircraft in the Arctic.

"Armed Forces search and rescue equipment has deteriorated," he maintained, "it is older, definitely not state of the art and it leaves a lot to be desired."

"If a major aviation accident occurs in the North," feared O'Connor, "there will be serious problems evacuating survivors due to obsolete equipment."

His concerns echoed those of the seasoned military man who spoke out to no avail 17 years earlier.

Describing members of the Airforce as "highly qualified and dedicated" yet "ill-paid and without proper equipment", O'Connor said there is a need for an investigation by Federal authorities.

As evidence of severely reduced search and rescue capability, O'Connor cited the 1991 decision of the Department of Defence — facing severe budgetary constraints — to ground the 'Chinook' which was the workhorse of Canada's helicopter fleet.

"Instead of getting rid of the Chinooks and eliminating search and rescue strength they (Federal government) should be increasing the priority they place on saving lives," charged O'Connor.

He called on the Federal government to give, "serious thought to the inadequacies of its air rescue equipment and to provide military personnel with the tools to do the job." He added, "they deserve it and will use it ... good people need good equipment."

An Armed Forces official agreed that the effectiveness of the search and rescue effort had been compromised to a weakened condition and hoped that the concerns being raised about the worsening state of affairs would, "force some people (Federal government) to make decisions ... to force them to examine the situation."

Another high-ranking officer admitted that, "there is a major flaw in the Armed Forces northern, mass evacuation plan." The senior member said supplies can be dropped into remote areas to sustain life for 360 survivors but rescue capability is severely limited because of the lack of helicopter resources to remove injury victims. He explained that Army and private helicopters could be commandeered but such action — time consuming when precious seconds count — is fraught with uncertainty. It is extremely worrisome, he revealed, to medical personnel who believe the plan is dangerous and will result in uncalled for death.

In relation to phasing out the Chinook helicopter, the top military official said although it was not used for small scale rescues such a machine would be invaluable in any airliner evacuation. Its loss, aging equipment, and the overall lack of helicopter strength, "makes a bad situation worse ... if they survive we cannot get them out."

In the meantime, the Officer in Charge of the Rescue Coordination Centre at CFB Namao said he would welcome a public review of the Armed Forces. Major Don Blair, a 30-year veteran, responded, "we're under the spotlight and accountable ... we're open to public scrutiny and if we don't get feedback we won't improve."

Those remarks preceeded the April 1991 resignation of the Vice-Chief of Canada's Defence staff. Vice Admiral Charles Thomas was quoted as saying his resignation was "a formal protest" with the hope that it would lead to a public debate on the entire defence issue. He expressed alarm that military equipment was continuing to deteriorate as it fell victim to age and rust. The concerns, perhaps coincidentally, were raised shortly after the Federal Government announced that it would spend $100 million on the Arctic environment. Put another way, the environment may be saved by a multi-million dollar project yet, as of this writing, there are no steps in place to ensure rapid removal of passengers from jet aircraft that crash in the inhospitable northern terrain. Survival experts rightly claim that anything less than quick removal of injury victims, particularly from the frigid Arctic wilds, is a sure guarantee of cruel and unnecessary death.

Considering the allegations made by Professor David Haley of a poorly equipped squadron with outdated equipment at the time of the Hartwell crash, almost 20 years previous, history brought truth to the expression, 'the more things change — the more they remain the same.' If the professor was the teacher it seemed that, unfortunately, the lessons were lost. Not only were they squandered but so were the dire warnings of a master in rescue techniques whose 1974 observations remain as valid today as ever before.

Nearly nineteen years after his death, David Kootook has not been honored posthumously by way of the Governor General's Award for Bravery. David Ward called it "a national disgrace" and said the decision to deny the young hero a fitting tribute should be reconsidered.

Marten Hartwell did return to northern flying. Ironically, he took to the air during the same week as the Hill family visited Spence Bay. It was less than two years after the crash.

The strength of Hartwell is best evidenced by the story of his life since that time. While Lewis Keseberg of the Donner party lived his remaining days in a pitiful state, Marten Hartwell has not.

He began flying again for a fishing lodge out of Cambridge Bay and settled with Susan Haley, who became his wife, at Fort

Norman, a community of less than 300 residents, in the Sahtu region of the Arctic. As much of the outer edge, with countless rivers and lakes in frontier territory, it is sought out by seasonal tourists from around the world. It is a kingdom, unspoiled by humans. In summer, it is known as 'the land of the midnight sun', with light, 24 hours a day.

Fort Norman was chosen as a place to live because the Slavey Dene, when others treated Hartwell as an outcast, petitioned him to make his home in their community.

Susan Haley, a dynamic woman with a hearty laugh, gave birth to two daughters and authored two books. Her second novel, 'A NEST OF SINGING BIRDS', was made into a network television movie. The non-fiction work that had been contemplated, the one on the crash that garnered worldwide attention, never materialized. For that matter, neither did a promised literary effort touted by famed novelist Mordecai Richler. He had received widespread publicity by travelling to the North and announcing plans to undertake such a task with the apparent agreement and co-operation of Hartwell. It never became more than talk. The award winning author's public pronouncement of writing a book on the subject never came to pass.

In October, 1987 Susan heard the sound of a Hercules search aircraft. Her husband had failed to return home while on a flight to drop off supplies for a trapper. She could not avoid the sinking feeling that he had again crashed and that he had perished. It was like a flashback to 1972.

The plane, a Cessna 185 with floats, as feared, had crashed. The pilot, however, again miraculously survived. One of the most controversial figures in Canadian aviation history had managed to live through yet another close brush with death.

Discovered, after he had stumbled through bush and snow for two days, Hartwell explained that the snow was falling heavily when he began his flight home and that visibility was extremely poor. The floats on his plane snagged the treetops, he said, and the aircraft plunged into the ground. He suffered sore feet and stiff thigh muscles, mainly from walking to safety, but otherwise was in fine shape.

He had not felt much like eating, he said, but if he had chosen to there were lots of rations aboard. This time he had been well equipped. Temperatures, hovering near freezing, were not a problem.

It was a time of delirious joy for Marten and Susan. He had survived on a wing and a prayer and he jokingly described himself as, "Captain Crunch."

She called him, "indestructible."

It was a happy ending and soon he was back in Fort Norman to a hero's welcome.

It led to a community feast with traditional songs and drums and cards and speeches.

"Welcome Home Marten — You Are The Best Bush Pilot", were the words on one card.

"A lot of times I've seen him when we were stuck in the bush and he took a risk to save our lives," a Dene woman told viewers of the Current Affairs program 'Focus North' on CBC television.

It had been 15 years since the crash of the mercy flight and Marten Hartwell again chose to publicly speak of it. This time, he did so through the medium of television.

There was no reluctance on his part to relate the details of the 1972 tragedy but when his dialogue voluntarily turned to his method of survival, the strain on his face and the halting, stuttering delivery of his words showed that the pain and the haunting memory remained.

His exact words, after contending that he did not know in 1972 how long someone could live without food, were, "the decision to, to, to eat human flesh was, was, was not, not very easy — absolutely, not easy."

I had the opportunity of meeting Mr. Hartwell in April, 1990. It was two and one-half years after that broadcast. I was employed to train journalists for the CBC and he happened to come in to the Yellowknife Inn, the hotel where the crash inquest took place, while in the city obtaining repairs to his aircraft. He looked fit and healthy. When I approached him and introduced myself, there was a very long period of silence. Our eyes locked and only then he responded with the words, "you caused me a lot of trouble." Knowing that he was referring to the story that first broke on CHQT years previous, I shared his opinion. Then, at my request, he ended a long pause by inviting me to join him. It led to a delightful conversation.

He confirmed the accuracy of his first words to his rescuers. We did not dwell on the subject.

He told me a story of his son who had departed a building shortly before a bomb hit it. He chuckled, describing his son as, "a survivor." His pride and sense of humor shone through.

The true survivor, white-haired and past the age of retirement, said he wanted to sell the air charter service that he operated out of Fort Norman. He joked, "maybe I could use some publicity."

His Dene friends call him "éhstee Marten" which, as CBC's Marie Wilson told her audience, "means grandfather — a term of endearment, honor and respect."

The Dene, the people of the land, truly understand the oftentimes cruel reality of life in the Arctic.

The land, at times, is harsh and unforgiving.

ITS PEOPLE ARE NOT.

Marten Hartwell and his partner remained hopeful in mid-May 1991 that they would be successful in selling Ursus Aviation Ltd. The company, which at one time boasted a fleet of three airplanes, had been reduced in recent years to a single craft. Whether it sold or not, confirmed Hartwell, their plan was to leave the North before year-end. He had a pension, he said, and he was finished flying. They intended to resettle with their young family on the Atlantic coast.

Fittingly, Hartwell's new chapter in life affords a natural close to the true but non-sanctioned story — THE SURVIVOR.

He once said, "I am not sure the choice to live was worth the years that followed. I look forward to walking down the street unnoticed — and I am almost there."

May he live in peace.

AIRBORNE — The survivor was back in the sky within two years of the crash. This picture was captured later, in 1978, as he refuelled his plane.

AGONY DISPLAYED — Hartwell as he recalled his ordeal in a 1987 CBC interview. It was 15 years after the Arctic tragedy. It was shortly after another aircraft wreck.

BOOK PROMOTION — Susan Haley, also 15 years following the fatal mercy flight, discussing her husband's 1987 downing of an aircraft. For CBC television, she also talked about her book on life at a university campus.

Edmonton Journal

FORECAST: BLOWING SNOW — EDMONTON, ALBERTA, MONDAY, DECEMBER 11, 1972 — 10c 15c with The Canadian and Color Comics

I didn't kill Neville — Brazilian

By JOHN LINDBLAD
Of The Journal

CURITIBA, Brazil — A young Brazilian, embittered in Canada because of broken dreams, Sunday demanded to face a secret informant who involved him in the Neville murder last year.

Elizaldo Luis Gonsalves, 27, located in his hometown by The Journal Saturday, categorically denied any knowledge in the June 13, 1971 murder of Bob Neville.

Journal reporter John Lindblad was assigned 10 days ago to find Elizaldo Luis Gonsalves after an informant in Edmonton implicated the Brazilian in the killing of travel agent Robert Neville. After talks with Canadian embassy officials and Brazilian government and police officials in Rio de Janeiro, Brazilia and Curitiba, Lindblad found Mr. Gonsalves, who denied the allegations. Lindblad talked with him about his life in Edmonton and Brazil and visited his home. The result is the accompanying story.

"I'm willing to go to Edmonton to clear my name. I will answer any questions. I will take a lie detector test or even truth serum".

Gonsalves, named "X" in a statement drawn up by a detective working for the law firm representing the man convicted of the Neville killing, Keith Latta, was reported to have told an informant — a man whom Gonsalves considered a friend while in Edmonton — that he had been paid $20,000 to kill Neville.

The statement, given to the attorney - general, has resulted in a request to Interpol to question Gonsalves.

(In Edmonton, the informant who had named Mr. Gonsalves said Sunday night: "My original statement about what Gonsalves said to me is true. However, I expected him to deny that he had killed Neville, if and when questioned.")

Brazilian police told The Journal they were drawing a portrait of a man with no previous criminal record. The official Interpol statement about Gonsalves was expected to take three weeks.

Gonsalves said he never knew nor met Neville or Latta and, contrary to the statement that implicated him, did not criminally flee Canada.

"I left Canada on June 25, 1971 with a broken dream. There was no hurry. You say a man was killed there on June 13 . . . I can't remember any murder then . . . Leaving 12 days after a murder is fleeing?" he said.

Reporter read statement

He sat in back of a Brazilian police car Saturday while I read the statement. At first he shook his head, almost giggled, thinking it was all a joke, and then literally gasped as he realized he was the man being described as a professional killer.

"Like a James Bond crazy thing," he said.

At a part of the statement which said Gonsalves had been involved in drugs in Edmonton, he sat speechless.

"I'm just a simple man. Who says these things? Why?"

When told part of the statement was based on a claim by Gonsalves's friend and an uncle of sorts to his children, he was on the verge of tears.

"Why? Why?"

He denied he had ever told the man even jokingly, that he ever said he was involved in any murder or drug traffic.

Gonsalves authorized The Journal to use his name. He said he was angry his name had become public through other media and asked aloud "They can say these things? Do these things?"

Gonsalves is in fact no mystery man. He lives in the same modest, three-bedroom home his family has had for 12 years. Once his correct address was learned and the house was found—a difficult job because of confusing buildings and the language barrier—Gonsalves was there to be found.

The name Gonsalves is as common here as Smith would be in Canada.

Catia Gonsalves, his wife, and his three children and mother were unaware of why The Journal wanted to see Luis Friday afternoon. They reacted first with pleasant surprise on seeing someone from Edmonton and then with growing concern on the arrival of a second Edmonton reporter, Peter Tadman, news director of radio station CHQT.

Edmonton post cards

In the first meeting, Mrs. Gonsalves made coffee and excitedly showed post cards from Edmonton. In halting English she said she had liked Canada. She said to return with an interpreter and said her husband would be home in hours. Upon return, a Brazilian police (federal) officer urged The Journal reporter to go away because the family was concerned over the sudden interest in them.

For Gonsalves, the whole thing "is like a nightmare".

Time and again over coffee in his home he would ask, "why?" and asked why the informant would say such things.

He wondered out loud about motives implicating him and thought they could range from money to jealousy.

The whole "crazy thing was like a wild police fiction story." For Gonsalves it was further hearbreak involving Canada.

He moved to Curitiba with his family as a child and after going to school took advanced courses in diesel engineering and industrial chemistry. He married Catia while working as a field engineer for Shell Oil in Brazil. They had two children, Maxine and Claudia, and in 1969 got "this dream of Canada".

He said he had heard good reports of Canada and its opportunities and was told by Canadian officials it was a land of promise.

The land of promise, he said, became a land of broken promises.

In Brazil, as established by documents he provided and police confirmation, Gonsalves makes about $12,000 a year. He drives a 1970 Volkswagen and would be described as middle class.

Job in oil industry

"When I go to Canada we arrived in Vancouver and went direct to Edmonton because the officials said with my skills I could get a job in the oil industry".

The land of promise never delivered.

He arrived in Canada with $2,500 and finally got a job after going to Ben Robinson at the Masonic Temple. The job was washing cabs for Yellow at near minimum wage. Three months later he changed jobs and worked as a janitor for a department store. He said his wife, then awaiting their third child, was nervous and confused because of language barrier and he asked for four days off to be close to her. When he came back to work, there was no job.

"And there I was. Broke with two kids and my wife awaiting a baby.

"It was the promised land, but suddenly it wasn't that much."

Gonsalves went to the Canadian immigration department and asked to be repatriated, he says.

The family went on city welfare.

He finally got a job as a busboy at the Chateau.

Gonsalves believes conditions in Canada prevent most

More GONSALVES Page 2

32-day Arctic agony ends for mercy pilot

Journal photo by Dave Roddie

Martin Hartwell at a press conference today

By STEVE and SUSAN HUME
Of The Journal

YELLOWKNIFE — Crippled pilot Martin Hartwell watched helplessly as his three passengers died one by one on the cold Arctic hillside where his plane crashed Nov. 8.

Thirty-two days of agony ended Saturday when he was rescued, eight days after the death of 14-year-old David Kootook, who had kept the makeshift camp supplied with firewood and gathered lichens to eat.

Mr. Hartwell, 47, in command of the Beechcraft 18 that vanished November 8 on a medical evacuation from Spence Bay via Cambridge Bay, watched his three passengers die following the crash into a heavily-wooded hillside 40 miles south of Sawmill Bay on Great Bear Lake.

With him in the twisted wreckage of the 10-passenger plane were the bodies of nurse Judy Hill, 27, Mrs. Neemee Nulliayok and her unborn child and 14-year-old David Kootook, all of Spence Bay on the Arctic coast.

After enduring cold that ranged to as low as 20 below zero and a starvation diet of melted snow, lichens and dextrose, a form of pure sugar, from Miss Hill's supplies when emergency rations ran out, Mr. Hartwell crawled from his crude shelter near the wreck to signal a passing plane.

Despite two broken ankles, a broken left knee and a smashed nose — all sustained in the crash — the pilot managed to hobble into the waist-deep snow to light a red emergency flare.

He was spotted as he thrashed around in the snow by Sgt. Bill Cheverre, watching from a Canadian Forces Hercules diverted to the area after radio signals from a crash location beacon were picked up Thursday night by a military aircraft not connected with the search.

Master Corporal Harvey Copeland and Corporal Al Williams, both paramedics from Edmonton, dropped into the crash zone from 1,000 feet, landing about three-quarters of a mile from the wreck.

Snow impeded rescuers

It took them an hour to struggle through the deep snow to Mr. Hartwell and the pilot was evacuated to hospital at Yellowknife by Canadian Forces helicopter just 90 minutes after the two men parachuted down.

He settled in at hospital for a supper of baby food — pureed chicken, mixed vegetables and banana custard — all his weakened body could deal with. His weight had dropped from 176 to 144 pounds.

"On the way back in he told us it was his birthday," Cpl. Williams told The Journal in an interview. "We asked him how old he was and he said he was zero zero, that it was the first day of his life."

Coroner Walter England, from Yellowknife, Sunday ordered the area within a 25-mile radius of the crash site be cordoned off. He, RCMP and ministry of transport officials were to leave for the scene at first light today.

The bodies of the victims were expected to be brought out from the crash site today. They will be flown to Edmonton to undergo autopsies under the supervision of Chief Provincial Coroner M. M. Cantor.

In a press conference at Stanton Yellowknife Hospital Saturday night, Dr. Warren Harrison said Mr. Hartwell was in "excellent physical condition for a man who has been isolated 31 days in the bush." He said the patient was not in the intensive care unit but was being treated in a private room on the ward.

The pilot showed no signs of suffering from exposure and had no frostbite in spite of the subzero temperatures. He was highly mobile when brought to the hospital helping to haul himself out of the ambulance.

Pilot heavily clothed

The doctor said Mr. Hartwell had been protected from the cold by exceptionally warm clothing — "a parka, two or three pairs of overalls, a heavy set of underwear and a heavy vest."

"He's suffering from malnutrition but that's all," Dr. Harrison said. "The way he felt he could have gone quite a while longer. He has accomplished quite a feat. He was so thankful to see that rescue plane he got down on his knees and went out to meet them."

Mr. Hartwell told his story in bits and pieces to the two men who rescued him but he refused to speak with any representatives of the press who were travelling to Yellowknife from all over North America.

The paramedics said the Beechcraft had been badly damaged in the crash with the wings and engines torn apart and the fuselage smashed.

"The airframe was a mess; it was completely

More CRASH Page 5
More stories and pictures on Pages 5 and 47

Hartwell offered money for story

Journal Yellowknife Bureau

YELLOWKNIFE — The bush pilot rescued from his crashed aircraft Saturday after 32 days in the open has hired a lawyer to handle the international bidding for exclusive rights to his story.

Brian Purdy said this morning he is acting for Martin Hartwell in dealing with offers coming mainly from the British press.

He said the offers run into five figures, and admitted agents from the London papers The Sunday Mirror and The People were arriving in Yellowknife today to negotiate.

"When Mr. Hartwell arrived in Yellowknife, there were a number of substantial offers waiting for him."

Mr. Purdy said the pilot "realizes his indebtedness" to some Canadian newspapers and broadcasting networks for providing the publicity that helped bring about the reopening of the search for his missing Beechcraft.

"He wants to make a statement to the Canadian press and the Canadian public.

"What I want to know is how far he can go without losing all these thousands of dollars for his exclusive story."

Eskimo boy, 14, proved a hero right to the end

Journal Staff Writer

YELLOWKNIFE — David Kootook started his brief and fatal odyssey as a boy and he ended it as a man.

The 14-year-old Eskimo boy from tiny Spence Bay on the remote Arctic coast died after clinging to life for 24 days in the frigid bush.

He died December 1 perhaps of starvation or illness, perhaps of something no doctor will ever find — a broken heart.

In the last three weeks of his life he faced a terrifying and brutal situation striving all the time to help the people with him who couldn't help themselves.

It overcame him in the end as death has a way of doing but young David thought of other people right to the end of his tragically short life.

"I would give the boy a lot of credit. Martin Hartwell wouldn't have been alive if it hadn't been for the Eskimo kid," says Master Corporal Harvey Copeland, a tough roughspoken medic who parachuted with Corporal Al Williams into the snowbound wilderness Saturday to rescue the pilot of a mercy flight missing since Nov. 8.

Cpl. Copeland was the first man to talk to the downed bush pilot after his 32-day ordeal in the wreckage of his Beechcraft 18 on the side of a hill south of Great Bear Lake.

The pilot was the only survivor and his rescuers pieced together the tale of David's determination and courage in the face of great odds from their scattered conversations with Mr. Hartwell and their knowledge of the crash scene and the survivors' injuries.

When Mr. Hartwell came to his senses near the shattered remains of his aircraft Nurse Judy Hill was dying and Mrs. Neemee Nulliayok was in serious condition because of her complicated pregnancy and a severe blow to the head.

The pilot was incapacitated with two broken ankles, a broken left knee and a broken nose. Only David had come through without any serious injuries and the boy went to work immediately moving the injured Mrs. Nulliayok and making her comfortable. It was in vain. She died five and half hours later following the death of Miss Hill.

The boy turned his attention to Mr. Hartwell. Together they managed to throw up a rough tent using a pair of engine tarpaulins and a piece of the aircraft, Cpl. Copeland said. "It was really comfortable for two people."

With the shelter up, the two survivors got a fire started and David worked at chopping wood to keep the vital blaze stoked up during the harsh nights where the tem-

More DAVID Page 2

Tot survives 240-foot fall

TOKYO (AP) - A traffic accident, a 240-foot fall and 31 hours of exposure to near-freezing temperatures — it sounds a fatal combination, but two-year-old Yuko Rikiishi survived it all.

She was rescued from beside a lake near here early today, police said.

Yuki was riding on her mother's back when a car swept by and killed her mother. The girl flew through the car's window on to the seat, suffering serious head injuries.

Police said a 21-year-old man admitted knocking Mrs. Rikiishi down and confessed he knew Yuki was still alive when he threw her over a cliff.

She fell nearly 240 feet on to a pile of leaves which partly covered her to protect her from the cold.

Where to find it

Ann Landers	18
Barry Craig	3
Birth, Deaths, Marriages	30
Bridge	34
Business, Stocks	50-52
Classified ads	31-45
Comics, Features	14
Comment	4
Crossword Puzzle	35
Entertainment	54, 55
Family Section	15-18
Focus on People	49
Health Column	19
Horoscope	33
Keith Ashwell	27
Letters To The Journal	4
News Digest	53
Patterns	33
Sport	21-26
TV, Radio	27
Wayne Overland	21

Weather

Intermittent snow and drifting snow today with winds northerly 15-20 and gusting, high 5-10 above, low 5-15 below. Cloudy Tuesday with temperatures rising steadily to 30 above. Details on Page 2.

They're on the moon . . . safe and sound

From AP-Reuter

HOUSTON (CP) — Americans landed on the moon today for the sixth and perhaps final time in this century. Apollo 17's lunar craft Challenger touched down in a rugged box canyon for the start of a three-day search for knowledge.

Astronauts Eugene Cernan, a navy pilot on his third space flight, and Harrison Schmitt, the first American scientist in space, guided Challenger over lunar mountains and down to the crater-pocked floor of the canyon called Tarus-Littrow.

Cernan and Schmitt will spend 75 hours on the moon, make three excursions in an electric car and collect about 200 pounds of rocks.

Apollo 17's third member, Ronald Evans, remained aboard the command ship, America.

Preparations for the landing went smoothly, with America and Challenger undocking and separating as planned.

They rocketed into orbit around the moon Sunday after a busy but uneventful voyage from Cape Kennedy, marred only by Cernan's digestive problems.

A perfect burn of the Apollo spacecraft's main propulsion engine first arrested its speed as it hurtled behind the moon, putting it into orbit, ready for the separation of the command ship America and the lunar lander Challenger.

While Cernan and Schmitt explore the fragile area of the moon's Taurus-Littorw region, America will continue to whirl around the moon performing a series of sophisticated experiments with pilot Ronald Evans in command.

Cernan and Schmitt, in three seven-hour excursions among the craters, hills and canyons of Taurus-Littrow, will walk and drive more than 20 miles over the valley floor searching rock and soil for secrets needed to complete the moon history already partially recorded through five earlier American landings.

America and Challenger, still locked nose-to-nose, swept behind the moon and out of touch with Mission Control at 12:36 p.m. MST Sunday. Eleven minutes later, they fired America's powerful service propulsion rocket engine to slow the speeding craft, and as it shot from behind the moon, from 250,000 miles away Cernan's voice crackled into the control centre:

"Thumbs up. America has arrived on station for the challenge ahead."

With their lunar goal at least near, the three spacemen let flow the joy and excitement of their view.

"We're breathing so hard, the windows are fogging up on the inside," said Evans.

Schmitt, the first American scientist in space, began a chattering catalogue of craters and mounds and shattered mountains, calling each of them by name.

Earlier, the spacemen ejected a 170-pound metal panel which had covered and protected the science instruments and cameras Evans will operate while in lunar orbit.

Two cameras will photo-

More APOLLO Page 2

FIRST WORD — A front page story about the rescue. Much more would follow before the last word.

UNCHANGED

NEARLY TWO DECADES LATER

— The inability of the military to quickly remove victims of major airline disasters in the North — an area covering one-third the landmass of Canada.

— The lack of a regulation requiring a final Emergency Locater Transmitter (ELT) check between pilots and towers.

— A flaw allowing sole eyewitnesses of death to avoid attending and being questioned under oath at inquests.

— Absence of recognition by way of the Governor General's Bravery Award for David Kootook.

The Young hero wanted his friends to know what had happened. Now they do.

NAMES

LEGAL

Cavanagh, James Creighton (Red)
Henning, Roy
Irving, Howard
Karswick, James
Ketchum, Philip
Morrow, Mr. Justice William
Purdy, Brian
Slaven, J.R.
Tingley, Everett
Trainer, William

MEDIA

British Broadcasting Corporation (BBC)
CHED Radio
CHQT Radio
Kane, Rhona — Toronto Sun
Lord Northcliffe — Observer/London, England
Flaherty, Gerald — Canadian Broadcasting
Corporation (CBC)
MacLean's — Canada's weekly
newsmagazine
Makris, Steve — Edmonton Journal
News of the North
Reidie, Dave — Edmonton Journal
Wilson, Marie — Canadian Broadcasting
Corporation (CBC)

MEDICAL

Boutin, Dr. Laurier
Brett, Dr. Harry Brian
Budd, Elizabeth Ann
Flatt, Dr. William Delanor
King, Julia May
Lapinski, Dr. J.J.
McCoy, Dr. Ernest

O'Donoghue, Dr.
Uygur, Dr. Ali Oktay
Walsh, Maeve

MILITARY

Bisson, Bob	— Master Corporal
Blair, Don	— Major
Connick, Dick	— Major
Copeland, Harvey	— Master Corporal
Desroches, Armand	— Major
Doucette, Fred	— Corporal
Gathercole, Keith	— Captain
Harrison, Dr. Warren Edward	
Howells, H.J. (Bud)	— Warrant Officer
Hayes, Austin	— Major
McPhail, Gary	— Captain
Moody, Ken	— Captain
Roe, Lance	— Corporal
Siminoski, Fred	— Captain
Thomas, Charles	— Vice Admiral
Toby, Neil	— Captain/United States military
White, Trevor	
Williams, Al	— Corporal

NEIGHBORS

Korpan, Lucille
Wolochatiuk, Glenn

NEWS SUBJECT

Gonzalves, Luiz Elizaldo

NOVELIST

Richler, Mordecai

PERFORMERS

Asner, Edward
Struthers, Sally

POLICE

Anderson, Robert	— Corporal
Feagan, Hugh	— Inspector
Fletcher, Robert Lauren	— Inspector
Kingdon, Ron	— Constable
Preston, Bob	— Constable
Pritchard, W.G.	— Superintendent
Tilley, Gerald	— Constable
Venner, Tom	— Inspector/Deputy Commissioner

POLITICIANS

Marchand, Jean	— Transport Minister, Canada
Nixon, Richard	— President, United States
Richardson, James	— Defence Minister, Canada
Trudeau, Pierre Elliott	— Prime Minister, Canada
Ward, David	— Alderman, Edmonton, Alberta, Canada

PRO-LIFE OBSERVERS

Landolt, Gwen	— Right to Life
Morris, Heather	— Alliance for Life

PUBLISHERS

Gorman, John T.
Donald-Gorman, Pamela

RELIGIOUS

LeMarier, Reverend Jean-Guy	— Roman Catholic church
Picketts, Reverend Willard C.	— United church
Scott, Archbishop E.W.	— Anglican church
Watchtower	— Jehovah's Witnesses

SURVIVOR

Hartwell, Marten (Herrmann, Leopold)

SURVIVOR'S FAMILY

Haley, Charlotte   Herrmann, Emmy
Haley, David   Herrmann, Peer
Haley, Susan

VICTIMS

Hill, Judith Ann, 27
Kootook, Davidie (David) Pessurajak, 14
Nulliayok, Neemee, 25

VICTIMS' FAMILY/FRIENDS

Brooks, Chris   Hill, Timothy
Hill, Eda   Kovalah, Johnny
Hill, Lawrence Jeffery   Lena

WITNESSES

Bigney, Sylvester Clyde
Brindle, Jock
Catling, Ronald George
Froehler, Alphonse
LaFleur, James
Logozar, Edward Gordon
McBurney, Brian
Medley, Ross Douglas
Murphy, Neal
Palmer, Edward Burton
Rae, Doug
Rainville, Marcel
Raymond, Gordon Dale
Thomas, David

REFERENCE

Mention was made in this writing to earlier authors detailing the will to live. For those who may be interested in reading their works they include:

ACROSS ARCTIC AMERICA, New York, Greenwood Press (1969) — Dr. Knud Rasmussen.

ARCTIC ADVENTURE, AMS Press/BOOK OF THE ESKIMOS, Fawcett/IVALU, THE ESKIMO WIFE, AMS Press — Peter Freuchen.

ART OF SURVIVAL, Dolphin Books — Cord Christian Troebst. Translated from German by Oliver Coburn.

HISTORY OF THE DONNER PARTY: A TRAGEDY OF THE SIERRA, Stanford University Press, 1947 — Charles F. McGlashan. An earlier 1879 edition is out of print.

HOWLING ARCTIC: THE REMARKABLE PEOPLE WHO MADE CANADA SOVEREIGN IN THE FARTHEST NORTH, Peter Martin Associates Ltd., 1970/printed by Alger Press — Ray Price. Several pages are devoted to MONICA ATAGUTTAALUK.

HOW TO STAY ALIVE IN THE WOODS, MacMillan — Bradford Angier.

SEARCH IN THE NORTH, St. Martin's Press — Guy Blanchet.

Printed in Canada